D0292290

How to Heal Toxic Thoughts

Other books by Sandra Ingerman

Soul Retrieval: Mending the Fragmented Self

Welcome Home: Following Your Soul's Journey Home

A Fall to Grace (fiction)

Medicine for the Earth: How to Transform Personal and Environmental Toxins

Shamanic Journeying: A Beginner's Guide

Audio Lecture Series (produced by Sounds True)

The Soul Retrieval Journey

A Beginner's Guide to Shamanic Journeying

Miracles for the Earth

How to Heal Toxic Thoughts

Sandra Ingerman

Sterling Publishing Co., Inc.
New York

Published by Sterling Publishing Co., Inc.
387 Park Avenue South, New York, NY 10016

Manufactured in the United States of America

ISBN-13: 978-1-4027-4260-6

To my husband, Woods Shoemaker, and my parents,
Aaron and Lee Ingerman

To the children of the world now and in the future:
May we leave you a healthy and peaceful planet
to live on so that you may thrive

Contents

How to Heal Toxic Thoughts

Once upon a time as the children were sleeping, a spell was cast upon the lands. When we awoke from the night, this spell had us believe that only what we could see in the physical world was real.

Under this spell, a magical, deep, rich, exciting way to experience life ended for all the children. For there is so much more to the world around us than what we can see with our ordinary eyes, hear with our ordinary ears, feel in our bodies beyond the sense of ordinary touch. And when we forgot this we forgot the magic of being alive.

As the veils between the seen and unseen worlds closed, children learned how to survive instead of how to thrive. They grew into suspicious adults who lost the ability to trust others as they forgot about the power of love. They learned how to manipulate others and to compete to get what they wanted.

But now the spell is wearing off. The adults who were once children are waking up and remembering the ways of the hidden world. And as new children are born, they come in and help the rest of us remember.

The time has come to wake up from the trance. Wake up now!

Introduction

One night I had a very powerful dream. I was standing around a water cooler with a group of coworkers. We were sipping our coffee and talking. The conversation seemed to be cordial, but I became aware that some of the workers were sending psychic "punches" to the others. I could actually *see* these invisible punches striking people in the solar plexus, and it amazed me. I would say to one who'd been punched, "Are you okay?" And then to the other, "Did you see what you just did?"

My dream made visible the invisible interactions of the hidden world. In waking life, exchanges like these are just as real—and all too common. When we observe how people behave, there may not seem to be any hostility. We may see a smile on the face of someone listening to us. But what is happening on an invisible level? What feelings are we triggering in him or her through our conversation or our presence?

We are more than our bodies, our thoughts, and our past experiences. We also have an invisible dimension that we call spirit—an aspect I like to think of as "who we are beyond our skin." We can't see this part of ourselves, but together with body and mind it makes up our whole being. And every time we interact with others in a visible, tangible way, on the level of the spirit an invisible exchange of energy is taking place too.

Each of us plays different roles in these exchanges; sometimes we are the senders, sometimes the receivers. And when the energy is negative, it can do harm just as physical violence can. Look at some of the phrases we commonly use to describe our daily dealings and how they make us feel. How many of them are associated with violent acts?

She's being pushy.
He's invading my space.
I felt beaten down.
She was worn down.
He was kicked when he was down.
She stabbed me in the back.
The whole group was held hostage by his behavior.
She was looking daggers at him.
The room was filled with explosive energy.
I made a suggestion but I was shot down.

The energy of violence acts on an invisible, psychic level, but it impacts both our physical health and our psychological well-being. We simply do not feel well on any level when we live and work in an environment that is thick with negative energy. You have surely been in a room where the fear or anger was tangible. You know it doesn't feel good to be there. You already know how toxic thoughts can be.

Since 1980 I have been studying an ancient form of spiritual healing called shamanism. The practice of shamanism dates back at least 40,000 years and, some anthropologists believe, possibly more than 100,000. A shaman is a man or woman who reads omens, divines information, and watches for signs in nature, working in partnership with the invisible and hidden worlds.

Shamans have taken on many roles in tribal communities, acting as healers, doctors, priests, psychotherapists, mystics, and storytellers. Historically, the shaman was responsible for keeping the community healthy, divining food sources, maintaining balance between the people and the natural world, and performing ceremonies to honor birth, death, and other life cycles both in humans and in nature. Today, shamanism is still practiced worldwide, and in some indigenous cultures the ceremonies and healing practices have been passed down through the generations unchanged. In other cultures, the practices have evolved to deal with emotional and physical illnesses traditional shamans did not face, including the rise of certain cancers due to environmental pollution and immune-deficiency problems such as chronic fatigue.

In the past, shamans were the doctors and psychologists of their communities. Today shamans work in conjunction with traditional medical and psychological practices. They look at the spiritual cause of illness—what is happening on the invisible level. Let's say for example that you had a diagnosis of cancer and went to a shaman in South America; the shaman would look at what was happening to you "beyond your skin," on the unseen level of the spirit. This spiritual diagnosis might explain that someone had sent you anger, causing your physical illness.

Before we developed guns and bombs, indigenous cultures used psychic warfare. They disempowered and overthrew their enemies by cursing them, consciously sending negative energy to those they wished to harm. Their weapons were thought-forms that could actually act as poison arrows, with the same effect as ingesting a poison into the body.

But all indigenous cultures understand that there is a difference between *sending* negative energy, such as anger, and merely *expressing* it. When someone expresses anger without sending out that poison arrow, he or she is simply acknowledging the feeling of anger, but the anger has no force or movement that could cause harm to another. In our culture, where we only acknowledge the visible—what we can see and experience on a tangible level—we deny this level of awareness, so we send our poison arrows unconsciously, not realizing the harm we do. This might be experienced by another as a slap in the face or a kick or punch. When you express a feeling without sending it, you simply state what you are feeling without a force behind it. What might be an energetic slap, kick, or punch is transformed by your intention to positive energy containing light and love, and this becomes the energy released into the room. In this way you are not harming another, but are also not harming yourself by repressing the energy you are feeling. Tools for working to transform the energy behind your thoughts and feelings will be given as you read on.

Here's an example of how this might happen. Let's say I am sitting in a meeting at work. One of my colleagues says something that triggers my fear that my job might be eliminated. But instead of dealing with my fear, I start to repeat to myself how much I hate my boss. Now I'm projecting anger silently but powerfully out into the room. The word *hate*, as I say it to myself, has a great deal of force fueled by the fear I'm feeling. The problematic energy shoots out into the room with as much impact as if I were punching and kicking everyone in it.

Think about this scenario and all the different ways it is played out by you and people you know every day. And think about how much problematic energy we are bombarded with day in and day out. Living in such energy is wearing us down—each of us individually and all of us together.

Imagine your hand. Now imagine that one of the fingers on your hand drops to the floor and believes that it has a life of its own, independent from the rest of your body. It sounds preposterous. But isn't this how we are behaving as humans today? We have forgotten what indigenous peoples and quantum physicists know: that we are not independent from the body we belong to, the web of life that connects us all.

From an indigenous point of view there is a spirit that lives in all things, and we are connected to this spirit, not separate from it. We are connected to everything that is alive. Trees, plants, rocks, clouds, rivers, oceans, stars, humans, animals, and insects are all part of one organism, interdependent, and we are related to all of these life-forms, not just to other humans. The energies of all of life link together into a web of life. A change in one part makes a change in the entire web.

Here's an example. Let's say in the area where you live there is a species of bird that eats a certain insect. If this bird becomes extinct, there will be no way to control the population of this insect. The whole ecosystem where you live will suffer.

Or think of it this way. Bees are responsible for pollinating flowers. As the environment changes due to the actions of humankind, bees are now being endangered. The environment in which they live is polluted and this is affecting their health. Without bees the sources of food for humans will also be in danger. There has always been a partnership between pollinators and plants; one third of all the food we eat comes from crops that require animal pollinators, a role often filled by bees.

These are physical examples of how the web of life works. But indigenous cultures also teach about our connection to an unseen web of life in which we are all connected energetically to one spiritual force. We give this force different names, depending on what religious or philosophical traditions we follow, but by any name it is the source of life.

You can use your body again to understand how our connection to our source works. If you break one of your arms, it is not just your arm that is hurt. Your arm is not isolated from the rest of your body. Your whole being is hurt. Every cell in your body is impacted. In the same way, we are part of a whole organism, and every action we take in life affects that organism. Every change we make in our consciousness ripples through the entire web of life. When we project toxic energy, it hurts all living beings. When we feel peace, it helps bring all beings peace.

For thousands of years spiritual teachings have said that our outer world is a reflection of our own inner state of consciousness. If you want to change the world outside, then you must learn how to change your state within.

If we look at today's environmental pollution from a spiritual perspective, we see that the pollution in our outer world is a reflection of the pollution in our inner world. This means that our toxic thoughts, feelings, attitudes, and beliefs are being reflected back to us by the pollution we see in our water, air, and earth. The energy from our negative thoughts and emotions is going into the water we drink, the air we breathe, the food we eat. And it is creating illness in others. But when we learn how to work through our negative thoughts, emotions, attitudes, and beliefs, we can create peace and well-being within us that helps to heal the world around us.

Gandhi said, "Be the change that you want to see in the world." I put it this way: "It is not what we do that changes the world, it is who we become."

In our work together, you will learn to identify your toxic thoughts, transmute their negative energy, and shield yourself from the harmful influences others are projecting out of ignorance. I will show you simple ways to transform who you are in the world so that you can become a true expression of peace.

This is an adaptation of a story indigenous traditions tell:

A grandfather was talking to his grandson about many things.

He said, "I feel as if two wolves are fighting in my heart. One wolf is vengeful, angry, violent, and the other is loving, compassionate, and strong."

The grandson asked the grandfather, "Which wolf will win the fight in your heart?"

The grandfather replied, "The one I feed."

Which wolf are you feeding?

Chapter 1

The Alchemy of the Soul

Many people today think that the old alchemists literally turned lead into gold. But in actuality they were working on a metaphorical level, changing lead-heavy consciousness into golden light. The word *alchemy*, from the Aramaic, means "working within and through the dense darkness inside." In this book we will use the ancient principle of alchemy to lighten the soul's darkness—to transform the energy you project in the world into love and light that can heal you and others.

The Power of Presence

I am sure you have met people you instinctively don't want to be around. They are like a dark cloud. But other people seem to lift you up just by being in their presence.

Here in the West, billions of dollars are spent "beautifying" the body, which is a rather shallow endeavor since there is a deeper beauty that we all possess. You've probably seen people who are not attractive as it's defined by magazines and beauty experts. But there is beauty in the light they exude and the way they carry themselves in the world. There is a peace, a still center, and a power that comes from within, felt by everyone with whom they have contact.

This ability to shine on those around us is something we all can achieve. We must turn our attention to healing our environment, the world, and ourselves by the light we shine. We must clean up the psychic environment we live in by learning how to transform our energy. This is what brings magic back into our lives. This is what makes us beautiful.

Our Reactive Selves

None of us wants to live in a hostile environment, but that is where we find ourselves today. Divisive energy is toxic. As our feelings of separation and division grow deeper, so does the toxicity around us.

As human beings we have egos, and the nature of the ego is to feel separate from others. The experience of feeling separate from others creates a host of emotions: anger, fear, jealousy, despair, violence, hate.

And because it's also human to compare ourselves with others, our interactions with the people around us touch deep nerves of self-worth and survival. We might feel that others have more intelligence, beauty, or wealth than we do. Our conversations with others might make us feel as if we are being judged. Our relationships with other people might lead us to feel "less than."

It is important to understand that having emotions is good. As conscious human beings, we are naturally going to have feelings about what we see, hear, and experience. And we need to express our emotions as a way to let off necessary steam—cancer research has shown that people who repress their emotions often manifest physical illness. We have a right to our feelings and thoughts; they lead us into the depth of consciousness where true growth can occur. But we want to allow our darker states of consciousness to nurture the seeds that new life springs from. We don't want to just stay stuck in the darkness.

In our work together we will look at practical ways to process the negative thoughts and emotions that come up throughout the day. We will learn how to express emotions in a healthy way, not just dump our negativity on others. In this way you can still feel your feelings, but the end product will be different. Instead of sending toxic energy to others and into the environment, you will learn how to send energy that becomes positive input.

Our Toxic Triggers

Our emotional reactions are set off by all kinds of triggers: the conversations we have with others, the normal issues that arise in family and other relationships, even outside events. We are often "triggered" when we watch the news. When we feel strongly about our values and opinions, we may be triggered by statements made and policies set by political leaders. If we are not allowed to fully express ourselves in work or school situations, we may feel triggered because our creativity is stifled. Which of these common triggers sets off an emotional reaction in you?

My family treats me like a child.

I felt humiliated when he brought up such an embarrassing story about my past.

I'm tired of my siblings competing with me for love.

I feel hurt when I'm told I should be more like my brother.

I'm so angry about the way the country is headed.

I feel so sad for all those people who lost their homes and loved ones in the earthquake.

I feel hopeless about all the injustice in the world.

I hate feeling judged by my boss.

My coworker's behavior just grates on my nerves.

The examples I gave probably stimulated a variety of problematic thoughts and emotions that you experience in your daily life, probably more often than you'd like to—perhaps even most of the time. We all have the bad habit of reacting and allowing ourselves to be triggered. And when we are in reaction mode all the time—when we spend our time trying to defend our opinions and shore up our self-worth—our senses start to become dulled and we cannot take in all that life has to offer. Instead of thriving, we often feel as if we are just surviving. When we have to protect ourselves all the time, we pay a heavy price.

We need to learn new habits for how we react to those around us. Think of exercising a muscle that you haven't used for a long time. At first it might take great effort to get the muscle moving with grace and ease. But as you build your strength and flexibility, the movement becomes natural.

In the chapters ahead, I will share techniques for changing your patterns of reaction and transforming your energy from negative to positive—simple practices that you can do anywhere and anytime, even while you are driving. And I hope you will feel inspired by what I share to come up with some methods of your own.

Take Some Time Out

What you've read so far has given you a lot to think about. Here is an exercise for you to use at this point to allow yourself to absorb and consider all the information you have just read.

Before moving on to the next section, I ask that you read through the exercise, outlined in the paragraphs that follow. Then close the book and sit in silence for a few minutes.

> *Start by just breathing deeply into your abdomen. Put your hands on your abdomen and breathe deeply enough that you feel your hands move up and down as you inhale and exhale. Take some slow, deep breaths. And just concentrate on your breath and your breathing for one or two minutes.*
>
> *Now allow yourself to reflect on what you have read. Notice what the material brings up for you. Just notice. You don't need to do anything with what you are feeling or thinking. But you do need to make a choice on how you want to proceed.*

Begin to answer the following questions. If you like, you can take some time now or later to write the answers in a journal.

Do you feel that there is any truth to what you have read about how unconscious we are of the energy behind our thoughts and emotions?

Would you like to do some personal work on this issue to find inner peace for yourself and to shine your own beauty and light in the world?

If you've answered yes to these questions, are you willing to commit to the work?

This work is an alchemy of the soul. It is a way of finding depth and richness in life and with your interaction with others. It is a way to change living in a superficial way to a life of more depth and beauty.

This is a practice that doesn't really take time, but it does take a willingness to stay aware throughout the day. It takes a commitment to work through the thoughts and feelings that come up for you. This work will take willpower on your part, for it takes a lot of willpower to stop the energy of a negative reaction moving in full force and replace it with a positive energy.

And, like all things that call for willpower, it will take practice, too. At first the task at hand might seem difficult for some of you, for in our culture we have not been trained to control our minds. But with practice you will find it easier and easier to work *with* your mind to create harmony and peace in your life instead of letting your mind get hooked into fear and anger. As you do the work outlined ahead, you will find yourself feeling more and more freedom to create states of consciousness and energy that empower you to change your own world.

All spiritual practices teach about the power of intention. When we set an intention, we set in motion the wheels of change in our lives. When we set an intention, action naturally follows. If you say yes to the commitment, then set an intention now. This intention will start to create the action—the way for you to change your way of being in the world.

One way to empower an intention is to tell someone else what you are planning to do. If there is someone in your life with whom you can share this work, tell him or her what changes you are getting ready to make in your life. If not, you might put the intention in writing, in a journal or a note to yourself, or simply set it in your mind and heart.

Chapter 2

Stop the Reaction

Think of your life as a garden. We all know how it feels to walk through a garden that has been tended with love. In our work together, we will look at ways to feed and nurture your garden of life and weed out what does not support health and growth.

As you learn how to transmute and transform the energy behind your negative thoughts, emotions, attitudes, and beliefs, the reward you find is inner peace. As you bathe in a state of love and appreciation, you experience energy that allows you and your garden to thrive. To do this, you need to break the cycle of triggers and habitual reactions that can make you feel trapped in your negativity. In this chapter you will learn how to tell when you're reacting and what you can do to stop the reaction.

Because our habits are deeply ingrained, this work may seem difficult at times. But remember, we are ultimately responsible for how we react and act. Open your mind to embrace your possibilities.

Connecting with Your Inner Peace and Light

Please do the following preparation exercise, which will take you about ten or fifteen minutes. Of course you can do it longer if you wish. First, read through the exercise so you can use it to guide your visualization. If you prefer, you might ask someone to read it aloud to you as you do the exercise. Or you could record yourself reading it aloud, then play the recording to guide you.

Next, find a comfortable spot to sit or lie down where you will not be disturbed. If you like, you can put on some music that is relaxing and peaceful to you. You might want to draw the blinds or curtains or place a scarf over your eyes.

> *Begin by placing your hands on your abdomen and start to breathe slowly. It doesn't matter if you breathe through your nose or mouth. What is important is that you take some deep breaths all the way down into your belly. Breathe comfortably for a few minutes, allowing your body to move into a deep and relaxed state. Allow your troubles and thoughts to be taken away by your breath. Feel your troubles and thoughts being transformed into pure light.*
>
> *As you continue to breathe slowly and deeply into your abdomen, think about a place in nature that you love. It is a place of great beauty or peace. It might be right where you live, nearby, or a faraway place you've traveled to.*
>
> *Experience yourself being in this place as fully as you can right now. Look around you and see all that there is*

to see. What are the colors, the plant life, the tree life, the animals, the birds, the fish? What life-forms inhabit this place? What does the sky look like? Are there clouds or is it clear? What is the color of the sky?

What are the sounds of nature around you? Does the wind make a sound or is the air still and silent? If there is water in this place, what is the sound? Is there birdsong here? What other life-forms are singing and communicating to you in this place?

Take a deep breath and take in the fragrance of the fresh, clean air. What else do you smell in this place?

Now feel your body sinking into the earth. The earth is holding you, supporting you, and loving you as it does each second in your life. Feel the air on your body. Do you feel it gently caressing you as it does in your life with each breath that you take? What is the temperature of the air? Do you feel the sun above you feeding you with the energy of life as it does each day of your life? Is there moisture in the air nourishing each cell of your body, as we all depend on water to nourish us on all levels?

Being in this place helps you to remember the preciousness of life. Being here now is a time-out from your busy life filled with activity and many thoughts. As you breathe, allow yourself to experience the peace and calm of being in nature as it reminds you of being connected to all of life. You are not just fingers living an independent life. You are connected to an organism of life that is always feeding you. You are connected to a web of life. As you breathe, deeply experience this connection.

Where did this great earth filled with such beauty come from? Where did you come from? What about other life-forms on earth? Consider the miracle of a body. It is such a complex makeup of cells that form organs, which have intelligence and give us life. We have a brain that allows us to experience this beauty and joy of being alive. We have the ability to create beauty and joy in our lives.

Some creator or creative force of the universe created us. Continuing to breathe deeply, experience your creator or creative force. Experience the love and light from which you were created. Experience how, like your creator, you also have the capacity to create love and light with your breath and thoughts.

Sink deeply into the experience of love from which this planet was created. Something so filled with beauty must have been created from pure love and joy.

Now put your hands on your heart. Listening to the sound of your heartbeat, experience yourself as more than just a physical body, thoughts, and life experiences. Allow your body to sink away into the earth. Travel deep within yourself until you experience yourself as just pure light.

You are a being of light. And you were given a body to experience the joys and wonders of earth. You can see beauty with your eyes. You can feel beauty with your body and with your sense of touch. You can feel the love of the sun, earth, air, and water. You can hear joy and beauty with your ears. You can hear the wind's caressing messages of love. You can smell the sweetness of life and taste the wonders of the food this great earth gives us in abundance.

With your mind you can create thoughts that go out into the universe and rain back down on you as creations from your love and light. You have the ability to manifest love and joy in your life. This is your destiny.

Now slowly dress yourself in your body again: cells, bones, organs, and skin. Embrace this body that has so much to experience, while at the same time remembering that you are a being of spiritual light.

Experience this place you are in with new eyes. Experience the depth of love and light here and the magic of life. Remember you have come here to experience and share love with all life-forms.

Remember; remember the truth of who you are.

As you continue to breathe with your hands on your heart, take one memory of being in this place and hold it in your heart. You might choose a symbol, a sound, a feeling, a smell, or a taste. Draw several deep breaths into your heart, embodying the symbol, sound, feeling, smell, or taste.

With your breath, allow your consciousness to bring you back to the room you are lying or sitting in. Come back with the memory that you are love and light. Hold in your heart the experience of life as precious.

And when you are ready, take your time, open your eyes, and experience yourself as fully present. You might experience a different vibration in your body. Breathe very slowly throughout your body. Allow your breath to fully ground you. Feel your breath moving through your feet down into the earth, connecting you to the earth. Feel your body on your floor, pillow, chair, or bed grounding you to the earth. Listen to the sounds in your room grounding you back home.

Discerning Your Truth

When we find ourselves facing conflict—with another person, with our circumstances, or within ourselves—we don't always respond to just what is happening in the moment. Consciously or unconsciously, our mind often attaches to some past experience that triggers a fear or survival reaction, such as the well-known "fight or flight," not related to the situation at hand. Part of our work is to learn to discern the difference between a real threat that warrants our attention and a perceived threat created by our mind. We need to learn how to rely on our inner knowing, our intuition, which comes from deep within, beyond the memories of our past experiences.

In the preparation exercise, you spent time experiencing your own inner peace and light, connecting with a source of truth deep within you. Now take a couple of minutes to try a more specific, very simple exercise to help you learn the difference between the thinking mind, which doesn't always give us accurate information, and the intuitive mind, which knows the truth.

Think about something that you love—a food, a flower, a taste, or a smell. Keep it simple. Go inside yourself, saying these words: I love __________. *Notice the sensations in your body as you tell yourself a truth. Do you perceive an image inside yourself when you do this? Do you get a physical feeling? Is there another sense that lets you know that you have told yourself a truth?*

Get up and walk around. Do a simple task to detach your mind and your senses from the experience you've just had. Then sit down again and this time tell yourself a lie: I hate ____________ *(the same thing you said you loved). Notice the feeling in your body when you tell yourself a lie. Does a visual image form? Does a different sense set off an alarm?*

Try doing the same exercise with other statements:

I want to live a life where I am fulfilled and healthy and know the truth of who I am. I am unwilling to settle for a life filled with superficiality.

I do not want to live a life where I am fulfilled and healthy and know the truth of who I am. I am willing to settle for a life filled with superficiality.

Notice how you feel as you say these different sets of statements to yourself.

Practice this over the next few weeks. It will help you learn to differentiate between the false fear triggered by a painful memory and the truth of your inner knowing.

As human beings we all have emotions. We all have problematic thoughts that come up in response to others and our environment. This is typical. We are working to transform the invisible energy *behind* these thoughts and emotions into an energy that embraces love and light.

Part of our growing process is to learn how to avoid reacting automatically. We want to have our experiences and work through our feelings, not just walk around the world reacting to everything that creates a challenge for us.

Our mind moves into automatic reactions very quickly. So it's important to learn how to stop these automatic defensive reactions when a trigger creates fear or anger. But how do we stop when the defensive reaction has become a habit?

Exercises to Stop Reactions

Here is one technique that I work with to stop myself from moving into a reactive state.

> *Come up with an image that is precious to you, like the face of a baby you know, or the face of a kitten or puppy. Picture yourself sending the energy behind your emotions to that precious being. Do you want to be sending toxic energy to someone or something precious to you?*
>
> *Take a breath and think about who's actually receiving your toxic energy. For example, let's say a telemarketer calls and disturbs you during dinner. Perhaps you had a bad day at work and your boss "dumped" on you because he was also having a bad day. On an unconscious level you dump all your aggressions onto this telemarketer. But the telemarketer is just trying to put food on the table for his family. Does he deserve to receive all this aggressive energy? Simply taking time to think this through—simply acknowledging the recipient of the energy—can stop the reaction.*

As you work to change your patterns of reaction, it's important to feel no guilt. The energy behind guilt is not healthy. Many of us have learned through experience that it's acceptable to kick others when we feel down. But when you allow yourself to get lost in the energy of guilt, you are essentially kicking yourself. An important part of this practice is learning to act lovingly toward yourself as well as others, since you, too, are a precious being that should not be harmed.

We are attempting to change our cultural conditioning and move to a new evolution of consciousness. This consciousness recognizes the impact our energy has on others and the planet: It is a consciousness of love. And making this shift takes work. The first step is to *want* to make the shift and to set an intention to do so. Once we set an intention, a change in our behavior will naturally follow. And learning how to transform our habitual reactions to others is an important part of that change.

Put Discernment into Action

Another method you might try using to stop a reaction comes from the truth-or-lie exercise I shared, in which you practiced identifying the images and sensations that come when you connect with (or deny) your inner knowing. This time, think of a symbol or feeling you can practice that will give you the message to stop, take a deep breath, and *not* react. Perhaps you envision a stop sign appearing as you are about to send negative energy. Or perhaps you feel a knot or butterflies in your stomach.

Once again, we are not repressing or denying our feelings. We are working all the way through them to turn them into something that will nourish our soul. If you have ever done any gardening, think about compost. When we compost consciously, beautiful flowers grow in our garden. When we don't work with our compost, it just sits around and rots.

Try an Experiment with a Plant

Here is a technique I use in my workshops to help participants become more conscious of the energy behind their thoughts and emotions throughout the day.

I bring to the workshop three-inch sod pots, soil, and herb seeds. I ask each participant to plant a little pot that will be a metaphor for his or her garden of life and to carry the plant around throughout the day, observing what energy is going into that garden.

For example, someone is at lunch with her little plant when the conversation turns into a heated political debate or moves into despair over the current climate changes. If she works through her feelings, the plant gets the energy of love. If she just sits on her feelings, simmers, and sends out anger to the person whose comments are triggering her problematic thoughts, this energy goes into the plant. So it would be this negative energy that ends up feeding her life instead of the energy of love.

Sometimes a participant actually puts a string through her pot and wears it like a necklace so that the plant lies on her heart. When she learns to transform the energy of her thoughts, attitudes, beliefs, and emotions into love and light, the seeds germinate very quickly. I have watched seeds germinate within two days when they are fed in this way.

Perhaps it's impractical for you to try such an experiment. If so, then you can buy a small plant to put on your desk at work or somewhere in your home where you will be around it a lot. Notice throughout the day the energy feeding your plant. This same energy is feeding your body and life.

You could also try this experiment with food and beverages. The energy you put into what you eat and drink is what you are digesting. Pay attention to the energy you're sending out while you purchase, prepare, or consume your food and drink throughout the day. What energy is feeding *you*?

Look in a Mirror

You could also try emoting while you watch yourself in a mirror. There might be some resistance to doing this; after all, no one wants to observe himself or herself acting out in a toxic way. But try it if you can. At some point you might start laughing at the absurdity of your behavior. This is good. One of the causes of toxic thoughts is that we tend to take ourselves too seriously. Bringing humor into our life creates a space for lightness and joy to permeate, and this creates healing.

Express, Don't Send

One day I was planning my errand route. I had one appointment I had to get to in the afternoon. I planned to run a large number of errands before I had to show up for my appointment. If the "errand gods" were with me, I could get all my errands done. But I left no room for any delay.

I was driving down a major street when the driver in front of me stopped his car to let a large truck turn out of a driveway. The turn was a tight one and would take many tries.

Now there was no way for me to complete all the errands I was determined to get done. My patience level was very low. I was leaving town in a few days and I felt completely stressed out.

It embarrasses me to say that this act of kindness by the driver in front of me moved me into a state of anger. I knew I was not being rational and that it was not a big deal that I would have to postpone some of my errands. But my adrenaline was really going.

I sat in my car and kept repeating to myself, "Express, don't send." To do this, I simply stated that I felt frustration that I could not finish my errands. This is a fact. At the same time through my intention I transformed the energy emanating from me to light rather than a force that contains a harmful psychic punch. As I did this I looked at the driver. He seemed like a nice man. Why would I even want to send poisonous energy his way? By using this kind of self-talk I was able to stop any harm going his way. By acknowledging my feelings I was able to stop my reaction and change my behavior.

Feeling stressed out can make us act in ways we might regret later on. Try repeating the motto "Express, don't send" as you find yourself losing patience over the actions of others. You might write it on pieces of paper and leave them in places where you might need this reminder. Leave such a note on the dashboard of your car or on your desk at work. Think of places where *you* need such a reminder.

Think of how much creative and productive energy can become available to you when you are freed from reactions to anger and fear.

Practical Ways to "Plant Your Garden"

We've looked at ways to stop your automatic reactions so you can feed your life-garden with positive rather than negative energy. You can extend the principle in practical ways into different areas of your life.

For example, I love to spin fiber into yarn on a spinning wheel. As I spin I think about spinning love into the yarn. In this way, people who wear what I make out of the yarn will be embraced in love. If you sew, crochet, or knit, you might want to consider the energy that goes into the clothes, scarves, afghans, and other creations that will be covering your loved ones.

When I cook or bake I think about how much I love the people I am preparing the food for. In this way they will ingest and absorb love. Think about what you are feeding yourself and your loved ones based on your mood as you prepare your food.

As I feed the wild birds and squirrels outside, I feel deep appreciation for the birds' songs and the animals' presence on the land. As I water my houseplants and my garden, I give thanks for their beauty so that I am feeding the soil and plants with love. You can do the same thing if you look at what energies go into your home as you do chores and repairs.

You can use this principle out in the world too. One of my daily errands is to go to the post office, where the energy is often thick with anger and frustration due to long and slow-moving lines. Part of my practice is to set an intention to lift the mood of the workers and customers who seem stressed out. I might do this by using kind words in conversations, by smiling at people, or just by sending out loving energy.

You can change what you "feed" your body, your home, your work environment, and your creative projects by raising your awareness and setting the intention to infuse love into everything you do. Use your imagination to think about places in your own personal and professional life where you might do this work. How do you want to plant your garden?

Chapter 3

Transmute the Energy

The real work begins once you stop reacting. The first step is honoring your thoughts and emotions, realizing that you are entitled to your feelings. The second step is acknowledging that you want to shift your energy. The third step is learning how to actually change the energy emanating from you into a vibration of love and light.

In this chapter we will look at specific techniques you can learn and use to transform energy, starting with the simplest of all: breathing.

Using Our Breath to Transmute

Back in the 1970s I worked for a temp agency and was assigned to different secretarial and office jobs. One of these was in a bank in a skyscraper in a very large city. My desk was on the same floor as the bank's vice president. The air in the office came through vents near the floor. Sometimes the air coming through would make the vice president's feet cold, so the air would be turned off.

By three o'clock each afternoon I was so oxygen-deprived, I would literally pass out at my desk. One of my coworkers would have to help me walk outside to get some air before I could go back in and continue my work. As the weeks went by, I found myself getting the flu a lot and finally had to quit the job. I loved the people I worked with, but the lack of oxygen was making me sick.

In our culture we just don't breathe properly, which is a major cause of both physical and emotional illness. I have a friend who was dealing with paralyzing anxiety for years. She tried to treat herself with various anti-anxiety medications, as well as alcohol, food, and other forms of escape, without success. Then my husband, Woods, who teaches meditation, yoga, and breathing, offered to show her some simple breathing practices she could try for five minutes a day. She immediately noticed that her anxiety began to lift. After a short while, she found that as long as she did the simple breathing exercises daily, her anxiety did not return.

Much has been written on breathing and how it affects our health and well-being. To be healthy both emotionally and physically, we need oxygen and we need to breathe correctly. For thousands of years, different breathing methods have been used to increase what the yogic traditions call *prana,* or life-force. Breathing is also a simple, effective way to transform energy. When you are in the grip of a reaction you may notice that your breathing is shallow and rapid, which may make your face feel hot. But when you are feeling centered, happy, or peaceful, you breathe with ease.

One of the benefits of breathing is to help you find your center. In fact, it is the easiest way to get centered when you find yourself being triggered by the words or behavior of others. Change cannot occur if we aren't centered.

Breathing can also help you stop the energy that goes into focusing on negative thoughts. When you breathe deeply, it can help you shift your energy from simply thinking to feeling more in touch with your body. Once you are more in touch with your body, you can access a state of deep inner knowing and move out of a reactionary state.

I have found that it's easy to get too hung up on the specifics of breathing practices. You can research different books on breathing later, if you choose, but for now I suggest that you might want to keep things simple and just be more conscious of how you breathe. You can start right now.

Try Some Breathing

Please read the next few paragraphs for some guidelines on conscious breathing. Then put down the book. You can remain seated or you can lie down. Close your eyes and place your hands on your abdomen. Take some deep breaths so that you feel your abdomen rising and falling.

Breathe through your nose or mouth. Most traditions teach that it is best to breathe through your nose. One East Indian yoga teacher says that as the breath moves through your nose and into your sinuses, a calming effect is created in your body. I have also worked with breathing exercises where people are instructed to breathe through their mouths. Find which way is more comfortable for you.

Breathe slowly. Rapid breathing is not a way to center; in fact, it might make you feel "spaced out" and ungrounded. There are breathing practices that do use rapid breaths to energize the body and are part of certain well-known spiritual practices. But here we are looking at how to calm the body.

If you haven't tried slow deep breathing before, you might feel a little disoriented. This is especially likely if you usually breathe in a shallow fashion. When we breathe shallowly, our energy contracts. When we breathe deeply, oxygen begins flowing throughout our entire body. The vibration of our body begins to shift, and we feel more expanded.

One of the benefits of allowing yourself to take slow deep breaths is that you will feel your own presence growing. And, once again, you will feel centered. If you do this when you feel triggered, you will notice that the energy you put out into the room changes. Others will notice it too.

A Calming Exercise

Here is a breathing exercise that you can use to create calm in the midst of a reactive mental or emotional state.

When trying to attain a calm state through breathing, you want to make sure your exhalation is longer than your inhalation. The teaching here is that to get a good inhalation, you actually begin by exhaling.

Begin by letting out air in a long exhalation. Then take a breath in and pause. Next, do a long exhalation. Now pause again.

There are a variety of ways that you can do this exercise. You can inhale on a count of four, pause, and then exhale as you count to eight. Or, instead of counting, you can repeat to yourself the word calm *or the phrase* I am calm *or* I am peaceful *during the exhalation.*

Different people find that different counts work for them. If it stresses your body to exhale for eight counts, obviously this will not be an exercise that produces a calm state. Experiment and see what way works the best for you.

Breathing to Create a State of Balance

In the last exercise you learned that to calm the body, it is important to exhale longer than you inhale. If you want to achieve a state of balance, use the same number of counts on the inhale as on the exhale, remembering to pause in between.

Here, as in the last exercise, you want to start with an exhalation. Then you want to find a comfortable count that works for you, somewhere between four and eight counts. Breathe in for four to eight counts, pause, and then breathe out for the same number of counts.

Breathing In and Through Your Heart

Another way of breathing to change your state of consciousness is to imagine yourself breathing in and through your heart. (You tried a little of this technique in Chapter 2 in the exercise for connecting with your inner peace and light.)

Actually put your hands on your heart so that you will feel your heart as you breathe in and out. Put an image or feeling of something precious in your heart as you do this.

I find that when I breathe in and through my heart, I have more access to my intuition. My energy moves from my normal state of mental chatter and reaction to a place of peace. I use this when I teach workshops. As I breathe in and through my heart, I find that my words come from a deep place of knowing.

People who have studied with me for a long time know when I am breathing through my heart. My presence changes significantly in the room as I shift more into an expanded state of consciousness and awareness. And the benefit for both my students and myself is that I am in a place of love and peace when I breathe through my heart, which affects everyone in the room.

A client of mine, George, was having a terrible time with his supervisor at work. Their chemistry was the sort that always seemed to cause an explosive reaction when they were together. Obviously their energies did not mix in a harmonious fashion.

I taught George the process of breathing through his heart while focusing on a precious image or feeling he had placed there. He practiced this for a while and noticed a shift inside himself.

One day, as a fight with his supervisor was beginning, he decided to try breathing through his heart. She was not aware of what he was doing, but all of a sudden there was silence in the room. The energy shifted, as did the conversation. For the first time, George felt a sense of compassion for his supervisor. Over time, as he continued to use this technique, his relationship with her changed.

Breathing is one of the simplest ways to transform any energy. When we are in reaction mode, our breathing becomes shallow. The more stressed out we become, the more we react. When we breathe deeply, the energy changes on its own.

Try some breathing while you are with other people. Notice how the energy in the room changes as you move into a centered and calm space. Notice how you can transform the energy in the room simply by breathing. Notice how your own presence moves from a contracted state into a more expanded state. Notice the sense of peace that you feel as you do this.

Take some time out to breathe now.

Working with the Energy behind Our Words

Words hold a tremendous amount of power. They affect our relationships with others as well as what we end up creating in the world, and they are powerful tools for transforming the energy we project. I see words as seeds. Every time we plant a seed word, it will grow. In the garden of your life, are you planting seeds of love or seeds of hate and fear?

Various ancient cultures understand the power of words and so treat them with great respect. The Navajo people have a saying: "May you walk in beauty." Whenever someone from the Navajo nation attends one of my lectures that includes a discussion on the power of words, he or she always comes up to me and explains the significance of the phrase. Essentially, it means don't say anything to another person unless it will create beauty in his or her life.

Hebrew and Sanskrit are what we call "vibrational languages." In Sanskrit it is believed that when you say a word, the vibration from that word goes up into the universe and comes back down as a physical manifestation. One Hindu creation story tells that the world sprang forth from the skulls of the goddess Kali's necklace. Each skull was a letter in the Sanskrit language. There are stories in the Hebrew tradition, too, about how words can be used to heal or to harm, to create or to destroy.

Hebrew is also called a consonantal language, meaning that it is made of consonants and not vowels. This is because the sounds and vibrations of the vowels are the real power; the consonants are what contain the power and therefore define the parameters of the power coming through. By not writing out the vowels, the language keeps the most powerful words secret. You have to be *told* which vowels are used in a particular word. Also, a word could be an extremely powerful word using one set of vowels, but an ordinary word using another set of vowels.

The Qabbalists say that the world was created by the letters of the alphabet, meaning through the use of sound and vibration. The Hebrew bible embodies the very sound of creation, the vibrations that actually were used to create and manifest. Therefore words are "creative," and if they are creative they can also be destructive. In ancient Egypt, action and words were often the same thing; words had so much power that often a metaphor was used in the place of a word. Otherwise it was thought that the energy of the word—potentially destructive—would manifest physically.

The creation stories of many cultures teach that the world was created with a sound or word. Genesis says that God created the world with the words "Let there be light." The New Testament says, "In the beginning was the Word, and the Word was with God, and the Word was God." In the cosmology of the Hopi, the sun god and earth goddess chant life into being. The Hindu scriptures teach us that *aum* is the sacred syllable from which the entire universe was created.

Even *abracadabra*, the incantation that many of us said as children, is actually a word of power that comes from the Aramaic. The original spelling is *abraq ad habra*, which literally means, "I will create as I speak."

What Do Your Words Create?

Here is a simple exercise to try. First, read through the visualization or ask someone to read it aloud to you. Or, if you like, make a recording of yourself reading it. Then get into a comfortable position either sitting up or lying down, either in nature or in your home. If you do this at home, you can put on some relaxing music that helps you move into an expanded place.

Think of a place in nature that you like to visit. This might be the same place you went to in the opening exercise of the preceding chapter. Find a nice rock or a place on the earth where you can sit. Experience yourself being there with all your senses alive and open.

Look around you and see all that there is to see in this place. Hear the sounds of nature around you. Feel the breeze on your skin and the ground or rock beneath you. Smell the fragrances here and taste the air.

As you sit in this precious spot on earth, start to say out loud some of the words you commonly use. Notice the vibration that travels out into the air and up into the sky.

Here are some words to get you started. Try saying the word brilliance. *Notice the invisible energy around this word. Now try saying the word* radiance *and notice what vibration is being sent out with this word. Try saying the word* hate *and notice the energy behind it. Now try saying* despair *and* pity.

As you sit in this place, try words you use in your own daily vocabulary. Notice what you send out and how it is affecting the energy field of the planet and the web of life. Notice what is raining back down on you as the energy you send out returns and manifests in your physical world. Notice what seeds you are planting in your garden of life.

Now as you continue this practice, try shifting your intention and notice if it changes the impact of the energy. Is there a different manifestation if you send the words I hate you? Notice how the intention behind your words fuels their power.

Practice words as long as you wish. When you are done, reflect on what you have learned about how to create a beautiful life-garden.

And when you feel ready, take some deep breaths and experience yourself returning to the place you are lying or sitting in. Allow your breath to connect you with your body and the earth. And when you are ready, open your eyes.

When I offer this exercise to my students, they're often surprised to realize how often it is not the word itself but the intention behind the word that makes a difference. In our culture, just as we don't look at the energy behind our thoughts and emotions, we don't look at the power behind our words; we don't consider what plants will grow from the seeds we plant in another person's psyche. At a conference, I led a group of health professionals through the same exercise you just did. I asked them to watch the vibration coming out of the words they used when they gave medical diagnoses to their patients. The exercise had a big impact on them as it opened their eyes to the effect their own words could have on their patients, not just at the level of information, but at a deeper level.

Using Words to Manifest Good

I have been working with the power of words since the early 1990s, and I try to be vigilant about the words I use in my workshops and with my clients. I always ask myself this question: Am I planting seeds of hope, love, and inspiration? Or am I planting seeds of fear?

This doesn't apply only to the words we say out loud to others. This same concept applies to our self-talk. A problematic state of consciousness can be drawn out and given force if you are using words that bring you down. If you say to yourself that you are not a good person and that you will never be able to create what you want, then that is exactly how your life will unfold. If you fill your mind with positive words, the energy and vibration will change in your life, leading to a positive manifestation. If you use words of hope, you will manifest hope.

Shamans are masters of the power of words. A classic shamanic healing practice in which the shaman uses words to cure the patient's illness is called *word doctoring*. Shamanic practitioners are also skilled at telling healing stories that open the patient's imagination to the possibility of healing.

For example, in my healing practice I try to inspire clients by sharing stories of how their lives can change in positive ways. Instead of focusing on past traumas, I focus on the gifts that have been returned to them during the healing. I might acknowledge that a client has had challenges in the past, but I focus on the good news that the ability to love has returned, or the ability to use creative energy has returned, or the ability to trust has returned. In this way, clients feel that there is hope to move forward in creating a better life that is filled with joy.

There are many brilliant doctors and psychotherapists today who are masters at word doctoring and telling healing stories. In a sense, everything a practitioner says to a patient is a sort of story; the key is whether the story locks the patient into a diagnosis or gives him or her inspiration and hope that growth and healing is possible.

Caroline Casey, astrologer and author of *Making the Gods Work for You,* says my all-time favorite line: "Imagination lays the tracks for the reality train to drive down." Our ability to heal and to change the environment we live in is directly associated with our ability to use our imagination to dream into being the world in which we want to live.

Politicians, religious leaders, and spiritual leaders can use this power to manipulate followers by instilling fear into a person's imagination. Or they can inspire by stimulating people's imaginations with unlimited possibilities. And it is all done through words.

Create lists of words that have the energy you want to manifest in *your* life. Try to use these words throughout the day. Notice how speaking these words out loud helps you feel more positive and creative.

On my desk I have Post-it notes filled with powerful words I wish to manifest. Some of my favorite words are *joy, awe, splendor, radiance, love, appreciation, light, magic, expansion, gratitude, wonder,* and *luminescence.*

I keep Post-it notes in my car with inspirational and positive words to help me when I begin to feel some road rage. At the moment my reaction arises, I see the words and realize that I have the choice and the power to stop my automatic, angry reaction.

I surround myself with these words so that I have easy access to them in situations likely to trigger a negative response. I conduct a lot of my business over the phone, and occasionally there are conflicts. During a difficult conversation, being surrounded by inspirational words reminds me that I can choose my response to the energies around me and my response can change the situation.

If I respond to conflict by using words that express the energies of love and peace, then that is the energy that follows. If I find myself reflexively engaging in conflict, creating feelings of hopelessness and anger in the other person, then those are the energies that will prevail between us.

Some of my students have worked with the power of words in business meetings. When a discussion becomes hostile, they counter with positive and inspirational statements that immediately shift the energy in the room. This is a useful reminder that while we usually can't change other people, we do have choices and those choices can transform our situations and ourselves.

The Power of Decrees versus Petitions

When we use our words to heal others and ourselves, we have a choice between using petitions and decrees. A petition is begging to ask for help. A decree is standing in your power with the understanding that all the help you need in life is available to you right now.

Sometimes we feel like petitioning for help; we feel powerless in a situation, down for the count. That is fine. It's just important to know the difference in vibration between the energy of a petition and the energy of a decree. Take a minute to notice the difference.

A decree might be:

I am love.

I am being held in the loving arms of my God, Buddha, Mary, Jesus, or the universe.

I have strong boundaries to protect myself from negativity.

I am strong.

I am whole.

A petition might be:

Please help me be strong.

Please love me.

Please make me whole.

Petitions ask for change to happen. Decrees help you make change happen; they help you transform energy because you are acknowledging that you already have all the help and tools you need.

I write decrees on index cards so I can look at them when I need strength and inspiration. I often paste one of these cards in my notebook or notepad to help me during a business meeting. I might choose one of the following phrases: "I am using my creativity to move this work in a positive and joyful direction." "All the support I need is here with me now." "I am surrounded and embraced with the love of the universe." These are statements of power that shift my state of consciousness. When I shift my state of consciousness I change the quality of my presence in a room. When I change my presence I can shift the energies around me. A decree is also an effective and powerful tool when we have a loved one who is suffering or when the suffering of others in a world catastrophe touches us. Often we respond to someone's suffering with pity, but that can actually rob him of his power to deal with the situation. Let's say that one of your friends has been diagnosed with cancer. If you respond from a place of pity and think to yourself, "You poor thing," you actually pull your friend down. If you think to yourself, "She is a strong person and has the strength, support, and tools to deal with this situation," you actually raise her up energetically, which empowers her.

I know a lot of people who don't let others know when they are being challenged by a life situation because they don't want to be pitied. I have friends and students who did not share when they were diagnosed with cancer because they were afraid that the fear and hopelessness put out by others in their behalf would turn into destructive energy that would take away the possibility of healing.

Today we see on the news heartbreaking stories of people who have lost loved ones, homes, and possessions in war or natural disasters. Of course we feel compassion for all who are suffering. But on this scale, too, pity takes away their power. When you find yourself moving into a state of pity for people who have suffered losses, try turning your feeling into a decree. You can say something like, "I see the light and strength in all those who have lost their loved ones or their homes." This is just one example. You can try out some other wording and see what feels best for you.

Because this is such an important point, I give my students the following example to fully understand it. Let's say that you are a facing a life challenge and you have communicated your challenge to the thousands of people reading this book.

Would you rather thousands of people around the world start to say, "You poor, poor person, I have such great pity for you"?

Or would you prefer to hear thousands of voices saying, "I know you can get through this time. I am sending you courage, encouragement, and prayers of support"?

When you feel as if you are in a hole, words of encouragement can help to pull you out of the hole. Words of pity, however well meant, can actually push you deeper in.

Writing Decrees

Let's take some time out and write some decrees. I will give you some more examples to inspire you.

Two thousand years ago, when Celtic soldiers went into battle against their Roman conquerors, instead of praying—"Please help me"—they would say, "The power of the sun is with me now." They would acknowledge the power they embraced.

Reread those two different statements and notice which one creates a feeling of strength for you.

Here is a Celtic prayer that uses decrees:

Deep peace of the running waves to you.
Deep peace of the flowing air to you.
Deep peace of the quiet earth to you.
Deep peace of the shining stars to you.
Deep peace of the Son of Peace to you.

Here is a decree one of my students sent me as a gift:

Power of the waterfall be yours.
Purity of the waterfall be yours.
Spirituality of waterfall be yours.

I keep his card on my desk where I see it every day.

The following decrees come from the Christian tradition:

The light of God surrounds me.
The love of God enfolds me.
The power of God protects me.
The presence of God watches over me.
Wherever I am, God is.

Find a quiet place that supports you while you practice writing out some decrees. You might want to put on some music. Or you might choose a place outside, where the power of nature can support you.

Write out some decrees that you can use in different scenarios.

When you watch the news and see a catastrophe where others are suffering, write down a decree that you can use throughout the day to empower them with the strength to face their challenge. Some examples might be: "I see you in your strength right now." "May you know that you are held in love by the world community."

When you receive a phone call from a friend or loved one talking about his suffering, write down a decree that provides the energetic help he needs to cope with what is happening in his life. Examples here might be: "The power to deal with your challenge is with you now." "Courage be yours now."

You can also write some decrees using words and descriptions from nature. Here are a couple of examples of decrees I have written demonstrating how the Celtic people might word a decree:

"Blessings of a strong oak tree upon you with deep roots that provide strength and the ability to stay centered in the midst of challenging times."

"May the blessings of the bear be yours as bear knows how to go within and heal himself when wounded."

Now write out some decrees that can empower you in *your* life.

You can try using a decree in your life by repeating it to yourself throughout the day, like a mantra. In Sanskrit, *man* means "mind" and *tra* means "freeing." So when you repeat a decree as you would recite a mantra, you are using words of power to manifest positive energy and power in your life and freeing your own mind at the same time.

Chapter 4

More Tools for Transformation

There are many ways to transform the energy you manifest in the world. In this chapter we will look at techniques that build on the tools we've already begun to use, as well as tools that use the power of symbols and the elements of nature.

Burst Your Troubles Like Bubbles

Songs, which combine the power of words with the power of breathing, have been used for thousands of years to promote physical and emotional well-being and to shift energy into a state of empowerment. When you really sing a song with gusto, you will find that your energy moves from your head into your heart. The oxygen moving through your song also awakens the rest of your body.

I feel strongly that many of us gave our power away to others when we were told that we couldn't sing. Some of us were told, as children, that our singing voice was so bad, it could hurt people's ears—and now we are too shy to open our mouth. But when we stop allowing music to flow through us in song, our energy collapses.

You can always shift your state of consciousness by singing something inspirational—either a piece you created or one you learned.

Santa Fe, New Mexico, where I live, has been in a drought for years. Every summer becomes tense as fire season approaches. I have to live with the knowledge that a fire could destroy my home. I have used all the work I've been describing to transform the energy of the fear I feel every summer.

Early one June morning, I heard on the news that the day was going to be very hot. I wanted to give some of my moisture-starved plants some help, so I headed out to water them. As I left my house to go to the garden, I saw that the sky was filled with smoke. There was a fire close by, and all my old fears started to fill up my energy.

I was reacting to the smell of smoke and the smoke in the sky. As I began watering, I realized that I was feeding my garden, which was already struggling, with the energy of fear. At that moment I made a choice to stop my reaction because I wanted to feed my garden with love, not fear.

So I started to sing a song I'd learned at a workshop about opening up and surrendering to light and love. At first I sounded pretty pitiful, as I was trying to force a state I wasn't feeling. But I continued, knowing that if I kept singing I would feel a physical and emotional shift in my body. And as I kept singing, the fear left my body. Energetically I moved into a state of surrender, just acknowledging that I wanted to share love and light with my plants at this moment.

After I finished watering, I went into the house to get something. When I came out I was singing the song softly, maintaining the state of openness that I wanted to hold. There was a jackrabbit in the garden munching the grass. As I passed the jackrabbit, he watched me and he showed no fear. He was cautious at first, then he went back to eating grass.

I felt that this was a great sign of how my energy had shifted. The rabbits that come to my house flee at the first sight or sound of humans. The fact that this rabbit stayed put while I passed by showed that my energy held no fear. When we can change our internal energy, all life is affected by the shift.

Think of a song that you already know. This is a song that lifts you up when you sing it by its beat, melody, and words. Find a song that feels energizing to your body. Sing it out loud when you are alone, or hum it when you are in public, to shift your state of consciousness. Notice how the world around you reflects your song of love and light back to you. Songs and music are healing, and this has been known for thousands of years. Plants, trees, animals, people—all life loves to be sung to. As time goes on, you might find yourself composing your own songs to shift your energy.

Simply Observe

Have you noticed that when you take a drive in the country, your observation of the scenery shifts you into a state of peace and calm? Watching the scenery change can also move you from thoughts of the past into focusing on the present moment.

Some spiritual practices teach observation as a way to change one's state of consciousness. From meditation to psychotherapy to physics, the underlying belief is that the presence of the observer—even the very act of observing—changes that which is being observed. Bacteria being observed under a microscope change their movement because of the fact that a technician is observing them. It has been found that the intention of the observer determines whether an electron exhibits itself as a particle or a wave. And when we are in a state of anger and we just observe it without trying to change it, our energy will shift too.

I have a strong part of my personality called "the observer." The observer will say, "Oh, you are feeling anxious right now. That's okay. Just experience that." This observer has been so helpful when I've needed to work through a state of consciousness. Sometimes I find myself so triggered by an event or conversation that my usual methods to transform the energy behind my thoughts and emotions just do not work. No matter how much willpower I put into changing a negative thought into a positive thought, I am simply stuck.

If I resist and tell myself I shouldn't be having these thoughts or emotions, I end up stoking the fire; resisting states of consciousness only makes the problem grow larger. But if I move into a state of observation and don't try to change how I am feeling or thinking, the energy is simply met and observed. At this point, the energy changes. During times when I can't control my reaction I repeat the following phrases to myself:

"I am very angry right now, and I need to experience this anger. I ask that the energy around my anger be transformed into an energy of love and light. I ask that no one be harmed, including myself, while I sit and work through this state." It may sound like a lot of words, but they just take seconds and they make a tremendous difference. This process allows my mind to do what it has to do while protecting others and myself from negative energy.

When I move into such a reactive state, the first question I ask myself is: To whom am I sending this energy? This question motivates me to ask for the energy to be transformed into light so I won't harm anyone. The same energy can feel toxic for my own body, too, so I use a decree that acknowledges I am being held in the loving arms of the universe while I change this lead-heavy consciousness into gold-light consciousness.

As I have said before, this work is a discipline requiring you to be aware of your habitual reactions. It takes daily practice so that it becomes a habit for you to stop reactions and to transform the energy you share in the world. To get to a place where you feel love, peace, and calm is a great reward. To get to a place where you feel that you are a being of light and then shining that light in the world is a gift to yourself and to those around you.

Embrace, recognize, and observe. The end result will be change, healing, and evolution.

We talk about body, mind, and spirit. The part of us that is spirit is who we are beyond our body, and our thoughts, and our past experiences. It is an invisible part of us that is pure spiritual light and exists in divine perfection at all times.

The Italian psychiatrist Roberto Assagioli, who lived and worked at the same time as Freud, believed that we are already perfect and whole and that the therapist's true role was to simply help the client remember this. In a form of therapy he developed, called *psychosynthesis,* he created many guided visualizations to help clients tap into their inner knowing.

In one, called the Disidentification Exercise, he leads you through a process to step back from what is triggering you and to experience that perfect, spiritual part of yourself. I put an adaptation of this exercise in my book *Medicine for the Earth.* There are also books on psychosynthesis where the whole exercise is written out.

I've done this exercise with many clients and have used it myself since 1982, when I was introduced to Assagioli's work while getting my master's in Counseling Psychology. I use a very short version to help me when I am in a triggered and reactive state. I simply repeat to myself:

I have a body, but I am not my body. I have a mind and thoughts, but I am not my mind. I have emotions and feelings, but I am not my emotions.

I can do this while I am driving and it works like a charm for me to disengage from a reactionary state. It helps me remember that I am so much more than the self-absorbed state I am caught up in. It reminds me that there is a beauty to life that warrants my good energy.

In the space that is created when I detach from the state of reactive consciousness I am in, I can breathe through my heart and feel love for the preciousness of life.

Take a few minutes to think about situations where this could be useful to you. And when your reactions arise, just give it a try.

Working with Symbols and Pictures

Carl Jung said that symbols speak to the unconscious and create change. A simple way of thinking about this is that, when we meditate on a symbol, a process begins in the depth of our being that we might not have an intellectual explanation for. A symbol or a picture can change our state of consciousness in the same way I described a song can do. It can lift our mood just by its beauty.

As we are so conditioned to react immediately to other people and to outside stimuli, it is important to surround ourselves with reminders that can help us break the habit. If you put a picture or a symbol up where you will see it a lot, it will be a powerful reminder to stop and not react. In my office I have many pictures and symbols that remind me that I want to create a sacred space that is healing for myself and others in my office and also in the world. Among them are pictures of religious and spiritual teachers who taught about the power of love and compassion.

I have a picture I painted of the light of my own spirit that reminds me of the truth of who I am. I have pictures of nature, such as flowers, trees, and stars, that keep me centered in my connection to all of life. They remind me that the energy I put out does affect all of life.

To stop your habitual reactions, put one or more inspirational pictures up in a place where you tend to lose yourself to negative thoughts and emotions. Put reminders on your desk at work and in your home to help you to remember, anchor into yourself a positive feeling. Put up pictures that make you smile and inspire a joyful state—perhaps pictures of loved ones or beautiful places in nature that you like to visit. Surround yourself with symbols such as hearts, the moon, the sun, the earth, stars, or your favorite flower that remind you of beauty and the preciousness of life.

And remember to keep singing.

Nature Heals Us

We are part of nature. We are affected by the change in the seasons and the cycles of the moon. As indigenous peoples put it, the earth has a heartbeat and we are one with the heartbeat of the earth.

But modern technology has separated us from the cycles of nature. We wake in the morning to an alarm clock instead of rising to the light of the sun. As we have electricity, we do not go to sleep with the cycle of the sun either. Our homes "protect" us from living in accordance with the change of seasons as, through the use of heat and air conditioning, we can separate ourselves from our outer environment. We look at calendars to tell us when the seasons are changing instead of watching the signs of change outside. Our cycles of activity and rest do not always flow with the cycles of nature, and we no longer connect with the heartbeat of the earth.

Irene is a doctor who works with people who have many allergies and have become very environmentally sensitive. She is a wonderful medical doctor who is also extremely intuitive.

Some years ago, a patient named Jennifer came to see her. She had been in a car accident several months before and had sustained a head injury. In the following months, her health took a nosedive and she developed multiple problems, including severe anxiety and environmental illness, which results when the stress of living in environmental pollution wears down our immune systems. Some people are more sensitive than others and have a greater impact from this environmental stress. These people can become allergic to fragrances, most food, and even the materials used to build homes and offices. Depending on the degree of environmental illness, some people have a hard time living in today's world. Jennifer was such a person. She could no longer work, and she had used up all her savings. She was desperate. Her friends chipped in for her to see Irene.

Irene took her history and gave her some suggestions. Jennifer told Irene she had no money to pay for any kind of treatment. But Irene wanted to help her, and she took some time in silence to see if her intuition had anything to offer. Then she told Jennifer to go live in a cabin in the mountains and lie on the earth every day—for at least thirty minutes twice a day, if not longer—rain, snow, or sunshine, until she was well.

Jennifer thought Irene was crazy. But she found a cabin whose owner needed a housesitter.

After about a year had gone by, Irene was at a party when a very extroverted and flamboyant woman approached her and started talking to her as if they were best friends. Irene asked her, "Do I know you?"

The woman was Jennifer, and she said that she had followed Irene's instructions. She had bundled up and lain on the earth every day and it had worked.

There are many stories like this of people who have overcome a variety of illnesses by moving into nature and living there until they heal. It goes back to the concept that we are not fingers separate from the hand, having an independent life from our own body or the body of the earth. We are part of a larger organism.

When we perceive ourselves as separate, independent fingers, we are cut off from living in the harmony and flow of nature. We separate ourselves from the nurturing we receive from the elements—earth, air, water, and fire in the form of the sun.

In physics, "coherence" describes a state of harmony as perfect as the phenomenon you hear when you are listening to an amazing symphony in which the instruments are playing so well together, you cannot separate them out. All the sounds are in concert.

When we are in a harmonious state where we experience in our bodies the connection with nature, the web of life, and our spiritual light, we too are in a state of coherence, all our cells communicating with one another in concert as in a beautiful symphony. It's when we experience ourselves as separate and we move into triggered reactive states or states of stress that our cellular communication breaks down and makes us ill.

Here are some techniques you can use to strengthen your connection with every element in nature and to transmute your energy into love and light.

Water Forms Us

Read the visualization below. When you are done, close your eyes and spend a couple of minutes in appreciation for the element water.

> *Before you were born onto this great earth you were just a little spark of light preparing to start a new adventure as a spirit coming to earth in a human form. And it is your destiny to learn how to be a spirit in a body who can manifest beauty and caretake this great earth.*
>
> *You found a womb to enter. While you were in the womb, water held you as you grew, protected you from any physical harm, and carried the nutrients from your mother to you, and as water broke, you entered into the world.*
>
> *Water continues to nurture you. You are mostly made up of water. The water you drink and the water that comes from the sky nurtures and cleanses you. You feel calm and peaceful when you are around large bodies of water; you love to hear the waves of the ocean and the*

sound of rushing rivers. Water reminds you that all life is about movement and change as you encounter it throughout the day.

When you feel as if you need to transform an energy that you are sending out, or you need to cleanse yourself of an energy you have taken in from others, you can use the life-force of water. You can experience the energy leaving you and being transformed into light while you wash your hands, or while you take a shower or bath, or while you stand in the rain. These are just some suggestions, and I hope I have inspired you to come up with your own way to work with water.

But please do not just dump negativity into this incredible living being. Instead, experience yourself letting go of the energy and then visualize the energy transforming into light as it travels with water back to the source.

Air Cleanses Us

After you read the following visualization, take a moment in silence to honor all the gifts of air.

It is often said that the first living being you bond with after leaving the womb is your mother. In actuality, the first living being you bond with is air. For your life begins with the first breath you take. And with each breath, you continue an intimate relationship with air.

Air is an incredible teacher of how we are all connected. When you breathe out, some of your DNA travels out of you and someone else breathes it in. So you are constantly connected with all of life through your breath.

Air is the last living being you say good-bye to as you leave your body and this great earth with your final breath.

Air gives us life and can also help us release and cleanse energies that we want transformed into light. If you feel the need to shift your state of consciousness, try blowing bubbles into the air. Envision the energy transforming into light while the bubbles carry your light into the world.

You can stand outside in the wind and let it cleanse you of any negativity you are sending or any negativity that you feel you have taken on. Again, as with water, you want to see what is being released into the wind as an energy of love and light.

Earth Supports Us

After reading this visualization, allow yourself to feel the power and appreciate the beauty of earth.

As you are born into a body, you are now connected with the great living body we call earth. Earth supports and holds you as you grow and live. Every step you take connects you with this great life-force.

You are nurtured by the incredible abundance of food the earth provides, and your soul is nurtured as you experience the extraordinary beauty of the earth and the life it supports. You are in awe of gems of all colors, flowering plants, gracious trees, and all the life-forms that are created on the earth.

The earth holds you and embraces you in love. When you feel you have energy to release, you can visualize burying it in the earth with great gratitude, asking that this energy be transformed into light and love. This light and love will seed the earth in such a way that you and others can continue to be nurtured.

Fire Transforms Us

After reading this visualization, take a moment to appreciate the power that the sun shares. Think about how fire brings new life into our lives.

> *There would be no life without the sun. Each morning for thousands of years, people around the world have given thanks for its return. Today we still honor the power of the sun. From childhood as you grew and started to play outside, you were energized by the sun, which is the element of fire. And still today the sun shines inside of you and this is your spirit. The sun shines above you, giving energy to all that is alive without asking for anything in return.*
>
> *The sun reminds you of your passion for life. As the sun shines brightly above you, generating energy to nurture all of life, your own sun shines within, fueling your creativity.*
>
> *The element of fire that burns teaches us about life and death. Fire takes what needs to be destroyed and always brings us new life, as with the seeds within the*

earth that need the heat of fire to germinate and burst forth in beauty.

Fire teaches you about transformation, regeneration, and the continual cycle of death and rebirth.

As you need to transform the energy you are sending or the energy you have taken on, you can use the energy of the sun. You might imagine putting the energy into a bonfire and having the fire, a natural transformer, shift the energy. Imagine yourself feeding the fire with the energy you wish to transform into love and light. When I do this, it works every time.

Chapter 5

The Nature of Projections

We are like the facets of a diamond. The many aspects of our personality are sculpted by destiny, and by our parents, siblings, family, teachers, and other authority figures, and by friends. We are shaped by the joys and hurts of our past relationships and experiences.

Many parts of our personality are available for all to see, but others are tucked away in secret places—both strong and wounded parts of ourselves. Many of us hide our inner light, for we were taught we would not receive love if we shone too brightly. Many of us hide parts of ourselves associated with times we felt we didn't belong and other experiences that bring up fear, sadness, and anger.

When we look into a mirror, even we don't see these aspects. But when we meet someone whose behavior expresses one of these hidden aspects of us, he or she can trigger a strong reaction. We may not even know these people personally; maybe we've seen them through the media or experienced them through their writing. But in situations such as these we can find ourselves projecting onto other people qualities that lie hidden inside of us.

We tend to blame others for our feelings, thoughts, attitudes, and beliefs. We also tend to idolize others without acknowledging that we have the same gifts and talents within, though we might express them differently in the world. And we also tend to project our own suffering, in the form of pity, onto others whom we think are suffering in some way.

For example, if you feel that you like how someone shines, it means you have that same ability but have not yet allowed yourself to express it. If you "hate" a personality trait in someone else, it means that same trait also lies hidden inside of you. Whatever you can see in others is also a part of you. When we are able to acknowledge our projections and experience parts of ourselves that are hidden, we stop sending so much of our energy to others. We embrace these parts that are carried within us. And as human beings we are here to learn, grow, and evolve. We are here to learn how to sculpt the deeply hidden parts of ourselves into a work of beauty, love, and light.

Examining Your Projections

Try the following exercise.

> *Take a notebook outside or find a comfortable place inside where you won't be disturbed. Write down the names*

of two people whom you put on a pedestal. Write down the qualities they express in the world that inspire you.

Now start to write a simple story about how you have these qualities buried within. Write quickly, without thinking, to unlock the hidden secrets buried in your unconscious. Try writing with your eyes closed or half-opened. Don't worry about how it looks on the page or how it sounds. Just keep writing. Just let your pen move without thought or effort.

Now try to do the same exercise with two people whom you really do not like or admire. Write down the aspects of their personality or behavior that trigger you, what it is about them you react to.

Take a deep breath. Now start to write a story about how these qualities are also facets of you that you have kept hidden. Don't worry if it doesn't have a beginning, middle, and end. Don't judge what you write; just allow what comes to flow through you.

The next step is to be able to look at people who trigger you from a place of compassion. You don't want to pity them, as this pulls down their energy, hindering their own process of evolution. But you also don't want to rationalize their behavior in the world. For example, if someone commits a crime that harms another, you want to have compassion for what moved him to a path of violence. And at the same time you might recognize that a violent streak lives in your unconscious. It does not mean it is okay to act out in a violent way. We all have choices about how we respond to our past abuses and wounds.

But it could be that this divine being has forgotten his spiritual light and hasn't yet found the tools to work through his wounds and remember his light.

Try moving into a state of love and appreciation for this person. Notice how your energy shifts. Experiencing love and appreciation for all of life is the most potent form of transforming energy I know.

Projecting Through Envy

We often compare ourselves to others, imagining that someone else has a better life, or a happier marriage, or a more satisfying career than we do. The truth is that this is pure projection.

The reason we project is that we don't always have an accurate reflection of ourselves. We cannot always see what we do have in life and who we really are. So we look outside ourselves and use others as a mirror, a basis for judgments about our lives.

I was giving a lecture with another spiritual teacher in a very affluent part of California. After our individual presentations we gave time for questions and answers. One of the comments from the audience was about how the people who lived in this area had more than others did. The assumption was that this affluence created better lives.

This comment was made several times, and each time I found myself feeling uneasy. Finally I needed to speak up. I have been teaching and working with clients in my healing and counseling practice for over twenty years. In meeting thousands of people, I have not seen that material wealth creates happiness. To the contrary, some of the wealthiest people I have worked with are also the unhappiest people I know. I have seen people who live in poverty who have a presence that lights up any room they are in. The quality of laughter in their eyes is the envy of those whose eyes are filled with emptiness and suffering.

This does not mean that I do not take issue with all the inequality in the world. What I am saying is that having material wealth does not always equate to a life of happiness. But this is the assumption we project onto the wealthy and famous when we envy what they have.

Some sense of competition can serve us well. It is often through feeling competitive that we strive to be the best we can be, so this can inspire us to keep working and growing.

But you know what deep jealousy and envy feel like. Jealousy might be a lover flirting; envy is desiring what someone has. And they hurt both your body and your psyche. It hurts the people you feel jealous and envious of, too, as you rob their energy. You may even unconsciously send toxic thoughts to them if your jealousy or envy leads to anger you don't express. Envy can become toxic in you and in the world. And I bet each of you has had a taste of this.

You've heard the adage that in life we can perceive our cup as half-empty or half-full. When we move into strong feelings of jealousy and envy, we are coming from a place of lack, from the experience that our cup is half-empty.

And yet creation comes from a place of abundance. You cannot create from a place of lack.

So what do you do when you move into this frame of mind, negatively comparing yourself to others? First you must remember that, like diamonds, we all manifest different facets of beauty and brilliance in the world.

I have never seen a group of people comparing the beauty of stars in the night sky. Nor have I heard people comparing the beauty of flowers. We might feel drawn to one flower over another, but we honor all flowers for the beauty they possess. We must treat one another—and ourselves—the same way.

We all have a destiny, but at the same time we also have the opportunity to make choices. We can create happy lives with what we are given. Or we can choose to be bitter over what life gives us. It is important for us to see that by the choices we make, we can grow, learn, and evolve.

The key to working through feelings of envy is first to acknowledge them, because they are a powerful emotion and should not be invalidated. At the same time, you don't want the energy to become toxic to yourself or others. What follows is an exercise to help you work through your projections by acknowledging your gifts.

Take a few minutes to go inside yourself, into a deep place of appreciation for who you are and how your life experiences have shaped you into the being that you are today. You are a star, and when you can recognize who you are beyond your thoughts and your body, you can shine your light in the world.

You have made a difference in the world through your life and actions. It is the small acts of kindness that you might have done on behalf of another—at work, in the grocery store, at school, in line at the bank—that truly show you have embraced your own brilliance.

When people near the end of life share their experience of reflecting on their lives, they say it is the small acts of kindness remembered that bring them comfort and peace. Can you remember just one small act of kindness that you have done on behalf of another?

The more you can acknowledge your own personal beauty and brilliance, the less you will compare what you have or what you perceive you don't have with others. The more you can appreciate who you have become through your life experiences, the more wealth you will feel inside. The more richness you feel in acknowledging your own strengths and beauty, the less you will look outside of yourself and compare yourself with others.

This requires taking some time each day to go within and reflect on what you do have and what you have done in the world. You can do this in the morning before you start your day. Or you can make it a practice before you go to sleep each night.

In time, you will create a peace inside that you wouldn't trade with another human being on the planet. And from this place of abundance you will begin to experience the unlimited possibilities you have to create in your life.

Projecting Despair, Pity, and Fear

In 2005, I spent about a month in Europe teaching and traveling. It was an extraordinary trip, and all my workshops went well.

But at the same time I was experiencing the joy of sharing my work, I was also facing some significant personal challenges. I was in Switzerland when Hurricane Wilma hit Florida, and I discovered that the media was not accurately reporting the extent of the damage. When I found out just how bad things really were, I became afraid for my ninety-one-year-old parents, who lived in the hurricane's path. For nearly twenty-four hours I suffered deeply as I could not find out if they were all right.

It turned out that my projection was not accurate at all. My parents were safe and being well taken care of. My imagination had led me to images of fear and suffering. But the deep sadness I'd felt over their unknown fate had opened me up emotionally. When I left Switzerland to go to Austria and to my next workshop, I caught some of the world news on CNN, and in my open and vulnerable state, scenes of the Pakistanis still living in tents long after the earthquake in their country hit me hard. On top of it all, in my conversations with the people I was meeting in my travels, I seemed to keep coming across stories of animal abuse.

As I flew from Austria to meet my husband in Amsterdam, I found that I was moving into a depression about the state of the world and the behavior of people toward one another and all of life. I found myself facing a deep, dark tunnel I had not experienced in many years.

There was no way around it. Entering into this tunnel seemed to be the next step on my path. I knew the tunnel was very long, and I also knew from my past experience that I would make it through. The only way out was through.

But as I felt myself getting ready to move forward into this darkness, I heard a voice from deep inside say that there was another choice, another way, another path.

I asked this voice to tell me more. It said I should remember that my external world is all a projection. It asked me: *What are you projecting onto all of life?*

Let's go back to the story about my parents. When I had no news on their well-being, I suffered deeply as I imagined them crying and in fear. But my projected picture of them was quite the opposite of their experience. They were happy and grateful that they were not harmed and that food and water was brought to them. They never felt any fear. They missed electricity, and hot water to bathe in, but that was a small price to pay for the fact that they were not hurt.

Just as I had been projecting the experience of suffering onto my parents, I realized that I was projecting a tremendous amount of suffering into the world. And I *did* remember that I had a choice. I also realized that spiraling into a dark depression did not help me, the planet, or the rest of life. I began to work with decrees to help me move out of the tunnel.

I recognized that if I wanted to be of service I needed to choose this new path. Changing my perception would change my reality. I had already written about this principle in *Medicine for the Earth*. And now I was having a deeper experience of my own teaching.

We can project darkness and suffering into the world. We can project hate and anger into the world. Or we can make the choice to project love, beauty, light, and peace into the world. During my time in Europe I was asked by the depth of my being to choose the latter, and I did.

The most creative forces in the world use the power of focus and projection. As a world community, are we tapping into this great power together? Can we be a greater force in the world by joining together our spiritual energies from a place of love for all of life? Can we change what we all project in the world?

Projecting Light into the Darkness

Let's say that you invited all the people around the world reading this book to project a perception onto you of what kind of person you are and what you are experiencing in life. Would you want that image to be one of a person who is suffering and should be pitied? Or would you like to be seen as a person standing strong in your divine light? Would you like a projection of being a person at peace with life? I suggest that you spend some time thinking about the power of projection. I have met many people who have traveled to indigenous cultures where people live in extreme poverty. But when one looks into the eyes of many of these people, a joy can be seen that is surprising. On one level, you can say, "These poor people—they have no homes and food to eat." Yet many of them carry a joy and peace that those who have an abundance of material wealth don't carry.

Is this a lesson for us: that we often project suffering onto others who are not experiencing suffering?

I am not saying that everyone is at peace with his or her life. But we also must look at how we project darkness in the world.

Millions of people around the world are projecting powerful energy onto others through their perception. Let us make a choice to gather our own energies together to consciously focus a projection onto the world that we would want projected onto ourselves.

We Always Have a Choice

All of us face challenges in life. We do have a choice in how we can react to those challenges. Some people who were abused in childhood grow up to be compassionate healers because they have made a commitment not to pass on the energies of abuse. Others who faced similar circumstances spend their lives in bitterness, perpetuating the abuse.

We can look to our own friends, family, and members of our community to see shining examples of people who have turned their lives around. These people came through very tough times and now inspire all of us with hope that we can do the same. We can also look to numerous examples of political and spiritual leaders who have turned their deep suffering around to be an inspiration to the world community.

Michelle Bachelet, the president of Chile, survived imprisonment and torture under the Pinochet regime thirty years ago. In her victory speech, she promised tolerance: "Because I was the victim of hatred, I have dedicated my life to reverse that hatred and turn it into understanding, tolerance and—why not say it—into love."

Nelson Mandela spent years in prison for speaking out against apartheid and racial discrimination. Since being released from prison he has traveled around the world inspiring people of all races. He speaks to the issues of equality, strength, and love.

The Dalai Lama was forced by the Chinese government to leave Tibet, his beloved home. The Buddhist people in Tibet have suffered severe religious persecution, yet the Dalai Lama teaches love and compassion. He is known throughout the world for his ability to move beyond bitterness and to teach about the power of forgiveness.

A student of mine told me an interesting story that gave me a lot to think about. It illustrates the way our perception creates our reality and underlines our choice to be bitter or grateful about what life brings us. This story was told by a woman from Cambodia who had to flee political persecution. She left with her family in the middle of the night. They had to escape so quickly, they could not bring any money or possessions with them.

They were starving and thirsty after days without food or drink. They finally came upon soiled rice and contaminated water. But the woman said they were so grateful to find food when they were hungry and water to drink when they were thirsty that they did not see the food or water as contaminated. There were no feelings of bitterness about what they had gone through, only gratitude for how they always found what they needed. They ate the food and drank the water and did not get sick.

You can choose to work with the power of projection to raise the spiritual vibration of the world by transforming dense, dark states of consciousness into lighter, bright states of consciousness. Start by thinking about what you would want a group of people projecting onto you. Then look at what you are projecting into the world. Would you like to change that projection?

This work involves working spiritually with changing the collective consciousness through the invisible and imaginal realms. It takes a great deal of focus.

We have to set a strong intention and come from a place of love. We cannot perceive ourselves as separate from the collective field around us. To project harmony, we must become harmony.

Tapping into our imagination of what is possible is crucial to this work. But the process involves more than mental imaging. You want to get your whole being involved. With your breath, feel yourself becoming peaceful, and with your whole being, project that peace outward. Become light and with your whole being project that light out into the world. Become love, and project that love.

Bring your children into this work. Teach them how to project light and peace into the world. This will help them keep light and hope in their own lives.

Chapter 6

A Time for Reflection

The work I am sharing with you takes discipline and willpower. It requires you to stay focused on your intention. You must have a vision of how you want to change your own life as well as the environment in which you live and work.

It's good to keep checking in on your progress. It's easy to stay focused about doing personal work when everything is going right. But when your body is hurting because of an illness, accident, or stress, you may find you become very weak-willed. When you are having a bad day, you may find it's easy to lose focus. And these are the times when you need focus most to transmute the energy of your own self-talk and the energy you are feeding others.

If you have ever watched or participated in sports, you know what I mean. When you are at the top of your game, performing well, it is easy to stay centered and "ride the wave." If you are dancing, miss a step, and don't immediately regain your rhythm, you lose your ground and your balance. But if you can take a deep breath, regain your center, and stand back up with grace, the dance isn't ruined; it takes on a whole new depth. In tennis, if a player is upset because of a bad call, he cannot get lost in his feelings about what happened. The game moves too quickly. He must focus, get positive, and stay centered in order to get back in the game.

At the end of each day, reflect on how well you handled your reactions, your thoughts, and your energy. How successful were you at stopping yourself from moving into a reactive state? How focused were you about shifting negative states of consciousness and changing your interactions with others? How did it feel to do the work? Did you notice a shift that felt rewarding for you? Did you change the environment you live and work in? How could you improve on what you did?

What Do You Feed?

To check how your day's work has gone, try this exercise.

> *Imagine two beings that can represent your state of consciousness. You might want to imagine two identical blow-up dolls that you pump air into so they get smaller or grow bigger. Label one the energy behind your positive thoughts, attitudes, emotions, and beliefs. Label one the energy behind your problematic thoughts, attitudes, emotions, and beliefs. At the end of your day, notice which doll looks plumper and which looks underfed. Which one did you feed more?*

This is an exercise for reflection, not for judging yourself. We are learning practices that can change our lives. We need to have patience with ourselves as we learn a new form of behavior while at the same time breaking bad habitual behavior. Remember, until we learn how to forgive ourselves we never really understand how to love others.

Being on a spiritual path is like walking on a fine rope. When you judge yourself, you fall off. The key is to get up, take a deep breath, find your center, and get back on the path and keep walking.

Changing Your Lifestyle

After working for a while on transmuting and transforming your energy, you will notice that you have become more sensitive on an energetic level. You'll be more attuned to other input that affects your energy and how you move in and out of reactive states, such as how much you exercise, what you eat, and how much stress there is in your life.

Delving into these topics fully is beyond the scope of this book. But I will encourage you to look at your lifestyle. For example, some studies have shown that foods that are high in fat can clog your liver, making you feel anger toward everything and everyone. For some people, too much caffeine creates a state of anxiety. Some substances, such as sugar, might create a state of emotional and physical depression shortly after you eat them. Eating foods that you are allergic to can also affect your moods, producing anger, depression, or fear. Begin tracking how you feel after you eat to discover the impact of different foods on your mood.

If you are stressed out all the time, it will be hard to stay centered. You might say that you cannot avoid living in a stressful way. But try to remember that when you first began reading this book, I asked you if you were willing to settle for a life where you survive rather than thrive. The only person who can change your life is you. Try to find simple ways to cut back on stress in your life. Start by making one small change where you let go of some stress. Notice the difference in your mood, your outlook, and the energy you send to yourself and out into the world.

Healthy bodies and healthy psyches need movement. We are part of nature, and everything in nature moves. There is a song in which the words say, "Earth is my body, water is my blood, air is my breath, and fire is my spirit."

Water that is moving is healthy. When water is stagnant, it becomes polluted. Air that is moving is healthy. Air that is not moving becomes stale. The earth itself is in constant movement. Our spirit, which is fire, needs movement or we lose passion and meaning for life. We stop being creative and fall into feelings of depression and despair.

Walk, dance, run. Do yoga or other forms of moving meditation, such as tai chi or chi gong. Join a gym or work out at home. You can find the time to take at least a fifteen-minute walk a day; it will clear your head and move the oxygen in your blood.

If you don't pay any attention to making lifestyle changes that support your physical and mental health, you might find that the work you are doing in this book only heals symptoms as they arise. To create real, lifelong change, you have to integrate the work you do on the spiritual level with the way you treat your body and your mind.

Effects of the Work

There are two main effects that you may experience as you get serious about doing the work of transmuting and transforming the energy you send out. As I've said, you may become more sensitive to the energies around you. But you will also stop perceiving yourself as a victim to the behavior of others. I noticed these effects after I first started writing about this subject in my second book, *Welcome Home: Following Your Soul's Journey Home,* which was published in 1993.

I took the work quite seriously. Every time I had a negative thought I would ask myself, "To whom did you just send that energy?" As I continued doing this, I found that psychically I was very open. I became acutely aware of my own energy and the energies around me. I felt like a new baby, thin-skinned, needing to take extra care of myself in my vulnerability. This experience was not bad, it was just new for me.

When we go about our lives reacting to the behavior of others and to our external circumstances, we end up always "stuck" in the times of our lives when things did not work out for us, tied to our old wounds and hurts. We are always being pulled back by our past.

You will find that, as you do the work of transmuting the energy behind your reactive states, you also make a choice to let go of your past. This is a big initiation. Initiation experiences create change in which you move into a whole new energy and vibration in your life. Initiations shape you into a new individual. You will be free of the past hurts that bind you. This will create an experience of living your life more in the present and creating unlimited possibilities for the future.

Although the pain of the past is uncomfortable, it is familiar. Now you will find yourself walking on an unfamiliar path as you free yourself from your past and work with states of consciousness that arise in the present. This is exciting work, and as you work through any fear that it brings up, you will find yourself moving forward to a life of harmony, peace, and beauty.

You will notice that you no longer perceive yourself as a victim to others around you or to your life circumstances. You always have ability to change your response to people and the energies around you. And this is a stance of power.

You will find yourself attracting new people into your life who reflect back to you your change in consciousness. You will find new situations being created in your life that reflect back the clarity that comes from staying in the present. You will thrive instead of just survive.

We are part of nature, and in nature there are cycles. The sun goes up and the sun goes down. Weather constantly changes. Storms come and go.

You will find that as you do your spiritual work you are also following natural cycles. There will be days when you feel great and so inspired about your new way of being in the world. And there will be days when you will fall into wondering, "What's the use?"

This is nature. And just as weather constantly changes, you can always rely on one thing: This too shall pass.

Don't get too hung up on the final result. Just stay in the present, in a place of love and appreciation for all you are experiencing and the great life adventure you are on. Just keep up the work; keep walking the path.

Chapter 7

Protect Yourself in a Toxic World

Travel back in time to visit a classic shamanic healing ceremony in Siberia. It is nighttime, and a bonfire is burning in the middle of the space where the shaman is doing her work. She is in a large dirt circle that is surrounded by pine trees. The air is pleasant, and it feels good to be outside. The stars and the beauty of the full moon light the sky. The shaman and her patient stand in a circle of village members who have come with the intention that their beloved community member will have a successful healing.

The shaman drums, dances, and sings during the ceremony. Hundreds of little mirrors sewn into her costume glitter as she sings and dances in the darkness of night. She also wears a belt with brass mirrors lining it. The mirrors reflect back any negative energies that might come toward her as she removes the illness from her client. These energies are sent back to their source with love.

As you do your work today, whether in a business meeting, in a healing session, or as you are out in the world, what can you use as a symbol of protection to deflect any hostile or fearful energies directed toward you? And how do you deflect them using the energy of love?

The Energy of Protection

We live in a world that is largely unaware of the energetic impact of thoughts and words. So far we've been examining what you can do to become more aware and in control of your own energy. Now we're going to take a look at what steps you can take to protect yourself from the negative energy of others.

Please keep in mind that if you become paranoid about needing protection, this is a form of toxic energy in itself. I have found that when people start to fear that they are being attacked on a psychic level, the effects of the attack actually grow stronger. There is no need to dwell in the fear that others can hurt you with their energy. You don't want to walk around all day in a suit of armor, but there are some simple ways to create a soft protective energy field around you. You have a lot of power in these situations to protect yourself. Here, we will look at some methods you can use.

I was lecturing on the issue of psychic attack at one of my workshops. After the workshop was over, I had a dream in which Jesus appeared filled with light. The light was shining through his heart and hands and out the top of his head. He proceeded to tell me that when you fill yourself with your own spiritual light and shine that light, there is no way for negativity to enter you or the space around you. I had discovered this myself over the years of working with the issue of attack and protection. But I felt this dream was a wonderful reminder that light is a potent way to protect ourselves.

Our evolution of consciousness is moving us to fully embrace the truth that we are beings of light and to shine our light in the world. The more you can experience your own inner light, your sun within, infusing each cell of your being, the more healing is available to you and through you to the web of life.

Using a Blue Egg

I was at a party in Berkeley during the early 1980s. There was a small group of teachers and healers present. Someone asked the group about ways that we had found to psychically protect ourselves.

One of the women there was from the Chumash, a Native American tribe from California. She told us how her people surround their energy fields in a protective blue egg. Blue is my favorite color, so I have been using this visualization method ever since. I have written about it in my books and taught it in my workshops and private sessions. The feedback I've received indicates that it's a potent method.

Let's say that you are in a helping profession, so you are impacted by your clients' energy. You want to encourage them to share the depths of their feelings and thoughts, but if you always take these energies into yourself, it could create burnout and even emotional or physical illness. To make sure you don't absorb the energy, imagine a blue egg of light surrounding you. In this way, whatever energy others share cannot enter your own field of energy. Some people like to imagine a white light surrounding them. Find a color that works for you. It is not the color that matters, it is the intention you set to be surrounded by a protective energy field. Remember: Your intention sets action in motion.

Using a Protective Symbol

Another way to work is to imagine a symbol that can act as a shield for you. You might have seen an image that you already know would be a great shield. Or you might sit with some crayons or colored pens and see what symbol comes to you. Set an intention to draw a symbol that you can use for protection and watch what emerges.

You can create a drawing or painting of this symbol and actually put it up in your office or where you meet people. Or you can just imagine this symbol sitting in your solar plexus area, shielding you from any negative energies coming your way.

The Protective Mirror

A method used in indigenous cultures when you feel you are vulnerable and need more help is to put a mirror under your bed. Anything coming to you during the night will be reflected back. I give this method to students or clients to use only when they feel they are under very strong attack, so vulnerable that visualizing themselves surrounded by protective energies is beyond them or does not seem like enough protection.

Protective Beings

I do a short visualization before I go to sleep at night. I see myself on the land, lying down beside a campfire to sleep.

Four tall firewatchers stand guard over me as I sleep. I can drift off knowing that I have protective forces watching my sleep space. I have found this to be very powerful, especially during the times when I have felt thin-skinned.

Fending Off Attack

Until now we've looked at ways you can protect yourself from unconscious negative energy. But if the negative energy is intentional, other methods are more effective. If you feel that someone has actually targeted you and is psychically attacking you, do not move into a state of fear. It is the fear, not the attack, that eventually ends up harming you. Remember, you are a being of light and you do have power. You don't want to retaliate and become aggressive and psychically counterattack someone you feel is trying to send harmful energies to you, lest what you send be returned to you exponentially.

Return to Sender

To deflect harmful energy sent with intention, I use the metaphor of someone sending me a gift in the mail. I look at the box and decide that I don't want to receive the gift. So I write on the box "Return to sender with love" and put it back in the mail. I make sure I am infusing the box with love so I am not sending back harmful energies. In this way, I am not doing harm to another, but at the same time I am standing in my power and not taking on other people's energy that is not mine.

Cut the Ties That Bind

As you look at creating harmonious energies in your life, it is time to reevaluate your relationships with others. You do not have to be anyone's psychic punching bag, whether those involved are spouses, lovers, family, friends, coworkers, or bosses or other authority figures. Being a psychic punching bag is not your job. It makes you a slave to another, and the days of slavery are over.

To declare your psychic freedom, develop your personal boundaries, and work on regaining your self-esteem, try cutting the energetic ties that bind you to people who don't reflect love back to you. These are not healthy relationships.

Imagine a cord from your solar plexus to a person you want freedom from. Imagine using a pair of scissors to cut the cord binding you to him or her.

Using the Power of Nature

You can use the same elemental exercises I suggested in Chapter 4 to clear yourself of attacking energies. Ask the power of nature to support you in transmuting any negative energy that has come into your space into love and light.

You can wash your hands or take a shower, washing away negativity and transforming all the energy that was sent to you into pure light and love. You can have the power of sun clear you or ask the wind to take from you that which does not belong to you. You can ask the earth to take any negative energies from you that need to be composted into fertilizer. You can do this as a visualization or out in nature.

Take the High Road

If you want to walk the high road, I will give you an exercise that you might find challenging at first but that will eventually lead you to feeling peaceful.

From a spiritual point of view, everything that occurs in the external world is a reflection of your own inner state. So think about this: When you feel that someone is psychically attacking you, it may be a reflection of your own behavior.

Spend some time giving this full consideration. It is a realization that does not come easily, especially when you have taken the stance of a victim and feel attached to your innocence. Take some time to walk outside and breathe deeply. Take some time to write down your thoughts about the recipient of your projections. Can you admit to any of this behavior?

If you do this, I promise you a peace that will be freeing. You will be so grateful that you were willing to undertake this act of courage and look at how your own behavior is being reflected back to you. Once you have identified this, you can go back over some of the earlier exercises in the book to work on your energy with a new perspective. Or you can look for outside help to discover the source of your behavior and work it through.

Experience All You Take In As Light

The more stressed out we become, the more vulnerable we are to toxic energy. Take time out to breathe. Learn to absorb the power of the sun, air, water, and earth. Take a walk in nature with the intention of absorbing the power of the elements.

From a spiritual perspective, everything is light. The food you eat is light, created from love. As you eat, experience yourself eating light and love. As you bathe and drink water, experience yourself taking in love and light. As you breathe, experience taking in the light and the love of air. As you feel the warmth of the sun, experience taking in the light feeding your cells and healing you on all levels.

If you adopt just this one practice you will find your health and well-being changing dramatically. Earth, air, water, and fire in the form of the sun give us life. Take in the power and light. Absorb it. It is a gift for you to receive.

Do the same with the light and the power of the universe. Take it in. Strengthen your body, mind, and spirit with the light of life. The light outside of you is also a reflection of your own internal light. As you become stronger, you will not feel so vulnerable to the negativity around you.

The key here is the ability to receive and absorb the light into your body and psyche. Think of yourself as a dry sponge absorbing water. Or think of yourself as a flower that has been in the rain for weeks: The sun finally comes out, and, as a flower, you soak in the light and warmth. If you like, you can find another metaphor to use that will help you fully get the experience of absorbing light.

Stories of Success

Jackie and Paul are married and they are both brilliant lawyers. As longtime students of mine, they started to work with some of this material when I wrote about it in my second book, *Welcome Home: Following Your Soul's Journey Home,* in 1993. They went deeper with the material as I wrote more on the subject in 2001 in *Medicine for the Earth: How to Transform Personal and Environmental Toxins.*

Over the years they have tried all that I have written here in their work with clients, in the courtroom, and at challenging times in their marriage.

Some methods they use more than others. They use breathing through their hearts while they listen to the stories of their clients. This prevents them from making judgments and helps them access intuitive knowledge on how they can best serve.

They both breathe through their hearts and visualize themselves surrounded by a translucent blue egg when the energy becomes aggressive in a heated courtroom debate. This helps them maintain a state of peace and calm in the midst of conflict.

They both work with the power of words and decrees when they speak in court. They keep putting out energy of love and light as they react to different courtroom antics and dramas. And they never pity their clients. They perceive their clients in their divinity, with the strength to deal with whatever the outcome might be.

They wash their hands at the end of the day, experiencing any toxic energies they have taken on being transformed into love and light.

Margo is a therapist who, when she began to work with me, was physically ill and exhausted from taking on the pain and suffering of her clients.

First I had to educate her about the ignorance in a modern-day culture of how one person's energy can be sent to another person and manifest itself as illness. Of course, in her case, the energies sent were not malignant. They came from clients who were working on themselves to become better people. In learning how to express themselves in the world, they were working through the wounds of the past.

I taught Margo the methods of protection that I have written about. This was useful, because she wanted to continue encouraging her clients to emote; she just didn't want to take their problematic energies into her own body and psyche.

Margo found that if she visualized a bright shining sun in her solar plexus, the sun could transmute any problematic energies that got into her field. She also liked using the translucent blue egg to surround herself while she worked with others.

More and more she has been getting in touch with her internal light and her divinity. And she has been excited to see that as she creates a loving and sacred space by the light she shares, her clients are responding quickly to her work and healing faster.

How to Clear a Space

There may be times when you feel you would like to clear a space of negative energies that have built up there.

There are many ways to do this. As always, the power of intention is important. Techniques and methods do not heal; love heals. As you can infuse any space you work or live in with love, you can create sacred space anywhere. And when you work in a sacred space, the love infused in it touches every person who enters the room; it lifts them up and heals them.

Breathing through your heart and infusing the room with love and light will always work to clear a space. If you like, you can try some other practices as well.

Candles, to most all of us, have some association with light and sacredness. We are used to seeing candles burning in holy spaces. You can light a small candle to represent the light being called upon to fill your space and keep it burning while you are working. The candle will reflect back to you the light within and without.

You can ask fire, a great transformer, to transmute and transform any energy in the space that needs to be cleared. You can close your eyes and visualize yourself putting energies in the fire that need to be transformed into light and love.

Some people like to burn incense to clear a space. The Native Americans burn sage, cedar, or sweetgrass as incense. In South America, copal and different forms of bark from trees are used. In Australia, eucalyptus leaves are burned.

But we are so bombarded with pollution today that many people's immune systems are deficient. This can cause an allergy to fragrances. I find that I can no longer burn incense at my workshops because of people who are allergic to the smoke or to the fragrance. Sometimes I will use a spray of rose water to clear the space before anyone arrives or after they've all gone. The fragrance does not linger.

And, obviously, at your place of work these methods may seem crazy to others. Here again the power of intention will work. You might want to bring in fresh flowers and put them on your desk to remind you that the space you are working in is sacred and filled with the light and love of the universe. Or you might want to hang an inspirational picture or keep a picture on your desk that will have the same effect.

However you decide to clear your space, begin by going deep within and experiencing your internal light moving through every cell of your body and pouring out of you. When you do this, you actually change the space you are in. You lift everyone up who comes into your presence.

Chapter 8

Toward a New Evolution of Consciousness

Imagine a world where, instead of watching the nightly news, everyone energetically checks in on the health of the whole web of life. Imagine a world where people gather their energies to heal the wounds of separation and infuse each strand of the web of life with light and love.

Imagine a world where you're walking down the street and someone accidentally sends you the energy of his thoughts, then says "pardon me," just as if he or she had inadvertently bumped into you or stepped on your toes.

Imagine a world where people have made the choice to walk the high road with the realization that all life is connected and that we must take care of this great earth that gives us an abundance of life. A world in which everyone as living beings understands the need to honor earth, air, water, and fire as the sun, and to hold all life-forms as equally precious.

Imagine a world where people join together in community to share resources and truly help one another, not just in times of distress but in the good times too.

Imagine a world where love and light are shared with each thought and emotion experienced. And where people see the spiritual light within and remember that we were all created from love and light, and we all shine as brightly as the stars in the night sky.

Use your imagination to call this world into being. Engage all your senses. See the scenery of such a world. Feel what it would feel like to live a life filled with love and light. Hear the sounds of people laughing and speaking words of love. Smell the fragrances in the air. Taste the tastes. Use your passion for wanting to live in such a world as fuel for your creation. And experience it as if it is already here now.

We Are Evolving

We know our perception creates our reality. Spiritual teachings throughout the world tell us that we create what we believe and that everything begins on a spiritual level before manifesting in the physical world. If we choose to perceive negativity, anger, and fear all around us, that will be our experience. If we move into a place of love and appreciation for all of life, our perception changes, creating light and love all around us.

Learning how to transmute the energy behind our thoughts, emotions, attitudes, and belief systems is a spiritual practice. Working with discipline on the words we use in our own self-talk and out loud with others is a spiritual practice.

When we look at who we are beyond our skin we find that we are spiritual light, source, creator, the creative forces of the universe, God. Experiencing all people as spiritual light and connected is the most powerful way to transmute and transform toxic states of consciousness.

As we bring these practices more and more into our lives, we will see a change in the physical world we live in. We will experience a world that embraces love, light, harmony, beauty, and peace.

I really believe that the stories the children of the future will read are not about one hero or heroine saving the world. The stories read to the children of the future are about communities of people gathering their energies together to change the world.

I find that most people are extremely open and receptive to the concepts I've shared here. But there are not many people who are willing to take on the discipline required. Many people I work with would rather maintain the illusion that their energy doesn't impact the world. And I am hoping that those of you reading this book will choose to become psychic warriors and help change the collective consciousness. When I say *psychic warriors* I am not using the term in an aggressive way. I mean that it takes the discipline, stamina, intention, and focus of a warrior to be successful at this work.

Our world and how the energy moves to create the future is in our hands. This is a gift and also a challenge. We can meet the challenge. No one else is going to make the world a better place to live in. We hold the power.

Always remember in time of conflict and change:
Stay focused.
Stay positive.
Stay centered.

Remember that every change in consciousness we experience, no matter how small it seems, ripples through the entire web of life. Each change you make changes the collective consciousness of the planet. Set an intention to integrate some of the practices written in this book and watch the beauty that manifests in your life and in the world.

After you finish reading this book, put the book down. Close your eyes and take a few deep breaths, keeping a precious image or feeling in your heart. Take just a few minutes in silence and experience the collective energy of anger, fear, frustration, and despair in the world being transformed into love and light. May this love and light bring light into all the dark places in the world. And may this energy of love and light rain back down on every living being, filling all with love.

Each day use this decree, or create your own:
Love and light is surrounding us and filling all of life now.

If you state a decree or do a short meditation like this for just a few minutes a day, you can start to change the collective energy of the world we share. We can create a loving environment in which to live and work. It takes all of us to gather our collective energies together to do so.

It is who we become, not what we do, that changes the world. Let us all set an intention to shine our light in the world and lift up everyone in our presence. This means while we are on line at the bank, the grocery store, or the gas station. This means sending our light into the world and changing the entire web of life. This means creating a world where we all thrive and don't just survive.

Find the light in you and let it shine. The world and the future of the world will change.

Go back to the story in the introduction of the Native American grandfather talking to his grandson about the two wolves in his heart. There are two hearts that are being fed right now in the world. There is the heart filled with love, light, unity, compassion, and respect for all of life. There is the heart filled with hate, anger, fear, and separation. Let's gather our energies together as a world community and heal the wounds of separation and feed the heart of love.

Blessings of the power of the sun be yours, filling you with light and vitality.

Blessings of the beauty of the night sky be yours, reminding you of the preciousness of life.

Blessings of the light of the moon be yours, reflecting back to you your spiritual beauty.

Blessings of the love of the earth be yours, embracing you with love and with deep inner peace.

Appendix

Frequently Asked Questions

Does this mean I can never be grumpy?
No. Just as there is stormy weather, there are times for feeling grumpy. Just transform the energy coming out of your grumpiness into love and light so that it is not hurting you or others. Then enjoy being grumpy!

How do I take back toxic energy I might have sent to a loved one?
Intention is key, as action will always follow. First, do not feel guilty about your human frailties. We are all here to learn, and learning is a process.

On a psychic level, ask for healing for anyone that you feel you might have harmed. See that person in his or her divine perfection right now.

Does this mean I have to like everyone? Isn't this being superficial?
Part of our work is to look at how others reflect back parts of ourselves we do not like. At the same time, it is true that we all meet people with whom our chemistry doesn't mix. You do not need to love or even like everyone. You can still experience him or her as a divine being. This is the real work.

Go back and do the work outlined in Chapter 5 on projection. You might make a choice not to spend any more time you need to with this person. But transform the energy around your judgments.

I have heard it said that there is no such thing as positive or negative energy—that all energy is neutral. Can you address this?

As part of the human condition there are different levels that we are working on simultaneously. As humans we often have to learn how to dance gracefully with the many paradoxes of life.

We live in a world of duality. The sun comes up and then goes down. It is not light or dark all the time. We judge things as good and bad, right and wrong.

But on a spiritual level there is only one web of life, one source, one light, one creative force of the universe. There is no good or bad; there is only energy.

A former student of mine is a master at working with this concept. She plays the cello in a symphony. She says that the audience arrives in a variety of states. Some people are tired. Some people have had a terrible day. Some people are angry or depressed. Some people are incredibly excited about being present at the concert. Some people are joyful about getting a night out with friends or a loved one. The list goes on.

My student says that she perceives this all as energy that she can absorb and use to be the best cello player. So if a person is sending anger, this is great energy for her to use as she plays. If a person is bored, this is energy available for her to use. If a person is happy, this, too, is just energy available for her to use.

You can only imagine the possibilities for all of us when we stop judging energy as good or bad and see it simply as energy that is available for us to use in our work and lives.

But we are starting with a modern-day culture that is deeply unconscious and ignorant about our energy and behavior. I feel very strongly that the first step is to teach people how to be more responsible for the energy they put out into the world, to understand how we react and act as victims, and to acknowledge how we blame others and our life circumstances for what is not working in our lives.

To skip this step would be doing a spiritual bypass. We have to do this work before we can be initiated into a new way of working with energy.

About the Author

Sandra Ingerman, MA, is the author of *Soul Retrieval: Mending the Fragmented Self, Welcome Home: Following Your Soul's Journey Home, A Fall to Grace, Medicine for the Earth: How to Transform Personal and Environmental Toxins,* and *Shamanic Journeying: A Beginner's Guide* (book and CD). She is also the author of the audio programs *The Soul Retrieval Journey, The Beginner's Guide to Shamanic Journeying,* and *Miracles for the Earth*—all produced by Sounds True.

Sandra teaches workshops internationally on shamanic journeying, healing, and reversing environmental pollution using spiritual methods. She has trained and founded an international alliance of Medicine for the Earth Teachers and shamanic teachers. Sandra is recognized for bridging ancient cross-cultural healing methods into our modern culture to address the needs of our times. Sandra is a licensed Marriage and Family Therapist and Professional Mental Health Counselor. She is also a board-certified expert on traumatic stress.

For more information on her work and a schedule of Sandra's workshops, please visit her Web site at: **www.shamanicvisions.com/ingerman.html**. On this site you can also read her monthly column, "Transmutation News." Sandra has published a few articles on her work at **www.sandraingerman.com**.

Please also visit her other Web sites: **www.shamanicteachers.com** and **www.medicinefortheearth.com**, where Sandra lists teachers of the spiritual work she shares in all her books.

If you are looking for a shamanic practitioner with whom you wish to work for spiritual healing, visit **www.shamanicteachers.com** and click on the "practitioners" link.

Acknowledgments

I give many thanks to my agent, Barbara Moulton, who continues to support my work and me, even though I typically stray from the norm.

I thank Patricia Gift and all those at Sterling Publishing who did such a good job in producing this book.

I would like to thank Anne Barthel at Sterling Publishing for her brilliant editorial help.

Nancy Sherwood (www.earthsea.ca) is the author of the story "The Two Wolves" in the introduction. This is Nancy's adaptation of an oral story told in many cultures. She generously allowed me to use her original version of the story. Thank you, Nancy!

Debra Chesnut was a great help, and I thank her for her explanation of how Hebrew is a vibrational and consonantal language.

I would like to thank Tom Cowan, author of many books, including Fire in the Head, for his help with Celtic history.

I am in deep gratitude to all the teachers and practitioners who trained with me and have formed an alliance to teach this material so the world becomes a harmonious and peaceful place for all of life.

And I wish to thank Woods Shoemaker and my parents, Aaron and Lee Ingerman, and my family for their continued unconditional love and support.

Index